The Future of Religion

THE FUTURE OF RELIGION

Richard Rorty and Gianni Vattimo

Edited by Santiago Zabala

COLUMBIA UNIVERSITY PRESS
NEW YORK

Columbia University Press
Publishers Since 1893
New York   Chichester, West Sussex

Published in Italy as *Il futuro della Religione. Solidarietà,
carità, ironia.* Copyright © Garzanti Libri, 2004

Library of Congress Cataloging-in-Publication Data
Rorty, Richard.
    [Futuro della religione. English]
    The future of religion / Richard Rorty and Gianni
    Vattimo ; edited by Santiago Zabala.
        p. cm.
    Includes bibliographical references and index.
    ISBN 0–231–13494–0 (cloth : alk. paper) —
    ISBN 0–231–50910–3 (electronic)
    1. Religion.   I. Vattimo, Gianni, 1936–   II. Zabala,
    Santiago, 1975–   III. Title.
BL48.R54 2004
200—dc22

                                                2004051913

♾

Columbia University Press books are printed on
permanent and durable acid-free paper.
Printed in the United States of America
Designed by Katie Chan
c 10 9 8 7 6 5 4 3 2

FOR PROF. C. ZUCKERT
WITH GOOD WISHES.

South
17-4-2009,

For Aldo Giorgio Gargani

CONTENTS

ACKNOWLEDGMENTS

I WOULD LIKE to express my gratitude to Richard Rorty and Gianni Vattimo, who accepted the idea of this book from the first, for taking a whole morning in Paris to answer my questions for the dialogue. Also, I must kindly thank the editorial staff at Columbia University Press, especially Wendy Lochner, Michael Haskell, and Jennifer Crewe, for their collegiality during the whole publishing process. Finally my debt of gratitude goes to Ugo Ugazio and William McCuaig, who revised the whole text and suggested important changes.

✳   ✳   ✳

The text by Richard Rorty, "Anticlericalism and Atheism," appeared first in Mark Wrathall, ed., *Religion After Metaphysics* (Cambridge: Cambridge University Press, 2002), 37–46.

The text by Gianni Vattimo, "The Age of Interpretation," was translated by Santiago Zabala. An earlier English translation appeared in *Between the Human and the Divine: Philosophical and Theological Hermeneutics*, ed. A. Wiercinski (Toronto: The Hermeneutic Press, 2002)

The dialogue "What Is Religion's Future After Metaphysics?" took place in Paris, 16 December 2002.

SANTIAGO ZABALA

The Future of Religion

A Religion Without Theists or Atheists

Santiago Zabala

> I cannot understand how any realization of the democratic ideal as a vital moral and spiritual ideal in human affairs is possible without surrender of the conception of the basic division to which supernatural Christianity is committed.
>
> —John Dewey, *A Common Faith*, 1934

> Rather I would suggest that the future of religion is connected with the possibility of developing a faith in the possibilities of human experience and human relationships that will create a vital sense of the solidarity of human interests and inspire action to make that sense a reality.
>
> —John Dewey, *What I Believe*, 1930

CONTRARY TO THE polytheism of antiquity, when gods did not manifest themselves without mediators, the Christian God donated his word directly to the community of the believers, instituting not only the "Age of the World-Picture" but also that of "two cultures," the quarrel between science and religion that divided the culture of the West into *opposing* sides: the natural and human sciences, atheism and theism, analytic and continental philosophy. Today, at the end of this epoch, we are witnessing the dissolution of philosophical theories such as positivist scientism and marxism that thought they had definitively liquidated religion. After modernity, there are no more strong philosophical reasons either to be an atheist refusing religion or to be a theist refusing science; the deconstruction of metaphysics has cleared the ground for a culture without those dualisms that have characterized our western tradition. In this postmodern condition, faith, no longer modeled on the Platonic image of the motionless God, absorbs these dualisms without recognizing in them any reasons for conflict. The rebirth of religion in the third millennium is not motivated by global threats such as terrorism or planetary ecological catastrophe, hitherto unprecedented, but by the death of God, in other words, by the secularization of the sacred that has been at the center of the process by which the civilization of the western world developed.

If the task of philosophy after the death of God—hence after the deconstruction of metaphysics—is a labor of stitching things back together, of reassembly, then secularization is the appropriate way of bearing witness to the attachment of modern European civilization to its own religious past, a relationship consisting not of surpassing and emancipation alone, but conservation, too. Contrary to the view of a good deal of contemporary theology, the death of God is something post-Christian rather than anti-Christian; by now we are living in the post-Christian time of the death of God, in which secularization has become the norm for all theological discourse.

It is in the "weak thought" of Richard Rorty and Gianni Vattimo that the new postreligious culture, which is to say the future of religion after the deconstruction of western ontology, is taking shape. In contemporary philosophy, Rorty represents the postempirical pragmatism of North America, and Vattimo, the postmodern direction of Latin Europe, as Michael Theunissen points out. From John Dewey's neopragmatism and Hans-Georg Gadamer's hermeneutics, Rorty and Vattimo both take not just the critique of the objectivistic self-understanding of the human sciences but also the concept of culture (*Bil-*

dung). Culture, according to Rorty and Vattimo, no longer stems from the assumption of a heredity but from an ever new self-description culminating in an existential self-creation that replaces the ideal of handed-down knowledge. "Weak thought" is an invitation to overcome metaphysics by involving it in a relation of reciprocity that is different from the Hegelian *Aufhebung* because "innovation" prevails over "conditioning." Overcoming the theological and platonic distinction between the "eternal and the temporal," between "the real and the apparent," between "Being and becoming" means that there exists an intermediate way between entrusting oneself to a divine substitute and entrusting oneself to individual preferences: this way consists of weakening and dissolving the ancient European concept of "Being" and the very idea of "ontological status." This new, weak way of thought not only opens up alternative directions, it also recovers tradition: the relationship between the believer and God is not conceived as power-laden but as a gentler relationship, in which God hands over all his power to man. Rorty himself says that in "a future Gadamerian culture, human beings would wish only to live up to one another, in the sense in which Galileo lived up to Aristotle, Blake to Milton, Dalton to Lucretius and Nietzsche to Socrates. The relationship between predecessor and successor would be conceived, as Gianni Vattimo has emphasized, not as the power-laden relation of 'overcoming' (*Überwindung*) but as the gentler relation of turning to new 'purposes' (*Verwindung*)."[1] Since the weight historically borne by the figure of God cannot be made to vanish by the deconstructive gesture of philosophy, we had better accept its historical influence and reconsider its presence with the appropriate irony.

Rorty and Vattimo start from the fact that before the Enlightenment humanity had duties toward God, whereas after the Enlightenment it also had them toward reason. However, both the "Age of Faith" and the "Age of Reason" traveled down the wrong road, not because they did not manage to seize the true nature of things, but because they did not take into account the importance of the new forms of life that humanity itself had in the meantime produced with a view to greater happiness. The present book starts from the position that humanity has entered the "Age of Interpretation," in which thought is dominated by concerns that do not pertain exclusively to science, philosophy, or religion. The new culture of dialogue inaugurated by Rorty and Vattimo invites us to follow, on the one hand, Friedrich Nietzsche, Martin Heidegger, and Jacques Derrida in their drastic deconstruction of the metaphysics of presence and, on the other, John Dewey, Benedetto Croce, and Hans-Georg Gadamer in going beyond that same metaphysics. The difference between these two groups is more a question of temperament and emphasis than one of doctrine. What unites all of them is the conviction that philosophical questions regarding Being and nothingness, language and reality, and God and his existence are pointless because they presuppose that philosophy can be practiced independently from history and that examination of our present way of proceeding might give us an understanding of the "structure" of all possible ways of human proceeding. For all these philosophers, objectivity is a question of "intersubjective linguistic consensus" between human beings and not some sort of accurate representation of something that transcends the human sphere. The ultimate goal of philosophical investigation after the end of metaphysics is no longer contact with something existing independently from us, but rather *Bildung*, the unending formation of oneself. This renovation of philosophy through the surpassing of metaphysics has a linguistic outcome in the idea that the linguistic a priori is the form in which our experience is structured. If this experience is essentially linguistic and our existence essentially historic, then there is no way to overcome language and to accede to the "whole" as reality. A passage from historical situatedness to a condition outside history is made impossible by the historicity of language itself, which always develops on the terrain of interpretation, in which there are no facts other than linguistic facts. "Hermeneutics," says Vattimo,

> is more than the *koiné* of the end-of-the-century humanistic culture and of the human sciences in general; it is also a true "ontology of actuality," a philosophy of that late-modern world in which the world really dissolves, and more and more so, into the play of interpretations. Insofar as it is assumed as a responsible historical project, hermeneutics actively grasps being's vocation of giving itself, and increasingly so, as the truth of human language, and not as thing and datum, *Gegenständigkeit*. It is by following this thread that it also finds the ground of ethical choices and it offers itself a true critical theory.[2]

The word "deconstruction" takes the measure of our whole stratified metaphysical tradition. This deconstruction, carried out mainly by Nietzsche, Heidegger, and Derrida, consists above all of retracing the history of western ontology destructively, in other words, the history of that conception, common to western metaphysics from Parmenides to Nietzsche, that identified "Being" with "beings." This deconstruction entails a speculative anamnesis of the history of thought, which does not aim to relativize the various conceptions of Being by referring them to the conceptual matrices out of which they arose in history but rather to isolate a common thread linking them, which Heidegger has called the "history" or "destiny of Being." This deconstruction of truth as intuitive evidence represents above all the end of logocentrism, that is, the end of the privilege accorded by metaphysical thought to presence and voice as incarnations of the Logos, capable of rendering Being available to a finite subject. In the course of this deconstructive assault on metaphysics, a sort of suspension of judgment, or epoché, has always been evoked, which leaves humanity without guidance and which ends by idealizing an unrealizable situation.

But what, for Rorty and Vattimo, are the historical events that have contributed to the deconstruction of metaphysics? The French Revolution (solidarity), Christianity (charity), and romanticism (irony). Thanks to these three events, the spiritual progress of man has consisted principally in the creation of an "I" that is larger, freer, and above all not fearful of losing the identity out of which it grew. It was Dewey's merit to have argued that we achieve full political maturity only at the moment when we succeed in doing without any metaphysical culture, without the culture of belief in nonhuman powers and forces. Only after the French Revolution did human beings learn to rely increasingly on their own powers; Dewey called the religion that teaches men to rely on themselves a "religion of love" (the complete opposite of a "religion of fear") because it is virtually impossible to distinguish it from the condition of the citizen who participates concretely in democracy.

Croce, for his part, in showing that "we cannot not call ourselves Christians," emphasized the necessary presence of Christian dogma and ethics in today's secularized culture. This position does no more than acknowledge how secularization has consumed the religious tradition of the West. Croce has taught us to look upon the secularized world as one in which weak identities mingle with the legacy of dogma left to us by Christianity; in other words, it is thanks to Christianity too that we are atheists.

Finally Gadamer delineates a contemporary culture of dialogue and fusion, in which "knowledge" is replaced by "*Bil-*

dung" (formation of the self or "edification"), in other words by a renewed awareness that not everything demands to be explained scientifically. In this way, religion becomes a universal ethos, an antidogmatic stance that constitutes the presupposition not only of hermeneutics but even of democracy itself. It is through developing its own laic vocation that Christianity can become a universal religion and promote the renewal of civil life. Thanks to Dewey, Croce, and Gadamer, in whom the history of objective spirit found more convinced defenders than in Nietzsche, Heidegger, and Derrida, religion may resume its role without masks and dogmatism, may once again take its place in the modern world alongside science and politics, without aspiring anymore to the absolute.[3]

The weak thought of Rorty's neopragmatism and Vattimo's hermeneutics inherits the task of the deconstruction of metaphysics: the *Verwindung* operated by weak thought aspires to a twisting continuation or tracking of the metaphysical tradition, as when an illness that has been overcome still remains present during the convalescence.[4] The difference between deconstruction and hermeneutics lies entirely in the modality of the overcoming: either one gets past metaphysics by showing that nothing remains of our past, or one gets past metaphysics by recognizing that this overcoming is itself a revisitation of the metaphysical past. It is easy to see how today's culture, governed by science, philosophy, and theology, has less and less to do with actual "discoveries"; its sphere is rather that of "analysis," according to the program of a purely linguistic analysis not determined by any ontological prejudice.[5]

According to Rorty and Vattimo, if truth does not occur at the level of facts but only at that of propositions, this corresponds to a cultural juncture at which the end of traditional metaphysics coincides with the dialogue between natural and human sciences, analytic and continental philosophy, atheism and theism; the meeting ground for this dialogue is language.

If the dispute between religion and science has gradually dissolved, it is because both parties have gradually taken their distance from the rationalistic motivations of modern culture and from its exclusive predilection for the problem of knowledge. As soon as one realizes, thanks to hermeneutics, that every critical thought comes about within a historical condition that makes it possible and supplies its substratum and framework—realizes, that is, the "historicity" of all knowledge—the division between scientific and humanistic culture becomes less consistent. To surpass metaphysics means, according to Rorty and Vattimo, to stop inquiring into what is real and what is not; it means recognizing that something is better understood the more one is able to say about it. Problems are resolved with irony, privately exercised vis-à-vis one's own predecessors rather than vis-à-vis their relation to truth.[6]

Wherever there is an authority that, in the guise of a scientific or ecclesiastical community, imposes something as objective truth, philosophy has the obligation to proceed in the opposite direction: to show that truth is never objectivity but always interpersonal dialogue that takes effect in the sharing of a language. Sharing a language does not mean sharing objectivities but agreeing on some preferences. The agreement reached through these preferences can give rise to a new paradigm, a new "language game" with the ability to free research from imprisonment within a single vocabulary. When Huxley, as Rorty says, challenged nineteenth-century Oxford in the name of empirical science, his intention was the same as that of Erasmus in his challenge to the academic institutions of his epoch—a challenge that aimed at surpassing the authority of intellectual institutions. The "skepticism" of Erasmus, made possible by humanism, and the "social hope" of Huxley, suggested by laboratory science, are not seen as progress toward truth, but as perspectives that humanity can reasonably prefer to others, new attempts by human society to resolve its own problems. This conception is common to both pragmatism and hermeneutics; indeed, both movements arose not merely in revolt against all authoritarian theories of truth but were also impelled by the intention to improve the way in which men understand one another.

Postmetaphysical thought fundamentally aims at an ontology of weakening that reduces the weight of the objective structures and the violence of dogmatism. The task of the philosopher today seems to be a reversal of the Platonic program: the philosopher now summons humans back to their historicity rather than to what is eternal. Philosophy appears dedicated more to the progressive edification of humanity than to the development of knowledge. This movement of thought might call to mind the Hegelian dialectic, were it not that in Rorty's and Vattimo's intentions the final vision of an absolute spirit, containing within itself the whole process, is absent; for the point is not to hold onto a place within traditional philosophy but to continue that conversation that since the beginning has characterized the West. Philosophy does not propose to demonstrate some truth but only to favor the possibility of a consensus that could be seen as truth.[7]

The principal characteristic of the "Gadamerian culture of dialogue" is no doubt the nihilistic and skeptical character imparted to it by the achievements of deconstruction. Truth of any kind is not attained with the help of "method," and in fact any idea of method is looked upon with suspicion. Rorty and Vattimo would not wish to be seen as bearers of new concepts, nor would they want to present their thought as anything more than a form of skepticism about all possible concepts, including the ones they themselves use and propose to us. Therefore, the analysis of today's philosophical direction outlined by John Paul II in his encyclical letter *Fides et ratio* is correct, although obviously it moves from the opposing point of view:

> Abandoning the investigation of being, modern philosophical research has concentrated instead upon human knowing. Rather than make use of the human capacity to know the truth, modern philosophy has preferred to accentuate the ways in which this capacity is limited and conditioned. This has given rise to different forms of agnosticism and relativism which have led philosophical research to lose its way in the shifting sands of widespread skepticism. Recent times have seen the rise to prominence of various doctrines which tend to devalue even the truths which had been judged certain. A legitimate plurality of positions has yielded to an undifferentiated pluralism, based upon the assumption that all positions are equally valid, which is one of today's most widespread symptoms of the lack of confidence in truth. . . . Hence we see among the men and women of our time, and not just in some philosophers, attitudes of widespread distrust of the human being's great capacity for knowledge. With a false modesty, people rest content with partial and provisional truths, no longer seeking to ask radical questions about the meaning and ultimate foundation of human, personal and social existence. In short, the hope that philosophy might be able to provide definitive answers to these questions has dwindled.[8]

Actually, the "assumption that all positions are equally valid" because "of the lack of confidence in truth" constitutes the greatest success obtained by the deconstruction of meta-physics.

With the end of metaphysics, the aim of intellectual activity is no longer knowledge of truth but a "conversation" in which every argument is fully entitled to find agreement without recourse to any authority. The space left open by metaphysics must not be filled up by new philosophies claiming to exhibit some foundation external to the "conversation." In contemporary culture, this position is represented not only by hermeneutics but also by scientists such as Thomas Kuhn and Arthur Fine, by philosophers such as Robert Brandom and Bas van Fraassen, and by theologians such as Jack Miles and Carmelo Dotolo, for whom the question of the demonstrability of the positions they maintain remains completely open because these positions are pragmatically and hermeneutically aimed at edification rather than knowledge.[9]

In the view of Rorty and Vattimo, secularization is nothing other than the history of weak thought: it is indeed secularization that teaches us that questions about the nature of God are useless because of the weakness of our reason.[10] We are not told that God does not exist, only that it is not clear what it actually means to affirm or deny his existence.[11] Postmodern man, who has lived out the end of the great unifying syntheses produced by traditional metaphysical thought, manages to live without neurosis in a world where God is no longer present, therefore in a world where there are no longer stable and guaranteed structures capable of supplying a unique, ultimate, and normative foundation for our knowledge and for our ethics.[12] In other words, postmodern man, no longer needful of the extreme, magical reassurance supplied by the idea of God, accepts the probability that history is not on his side at all and that there is no power capable of guaranteeing him the happiness he seeks. Postmodern man has thus learned to live without anxiety in the relative world of half-truths. The ideal of an absolute certainty, of a totally founded knowledge and of a world rationally arranged is for him only a reassuring myth proper to humanity's early stages, when powerlessness and fear in the face of the forces of nature became the predominant outlook and ended, as the old saying went, by creating the gods. Thanks to secularization, man breaks free of the hierarchy of creation and from all limits, whether those of cosmology (as predicated in the Greek vision of the world) or those of theology (as predicated by the Church). In this sense, would a weak concept of reason no longer be consonant with the evangelic preaching of love? Paul himself does not hesitate to affirm "when I'm weak that's when I'm strong." It is the fragmentation of reason, typical of postmodern thought, that provides man with an open space in which, to avoid getting entangled any more in contradictions, the Church ought henceforth to proclaim its own message of faith.

This man of postmodernity, if he submits fully to the weak condition of Being and of existence, may finally learn to live together with himself and with his own finitude, apart from any residual nostalgia for the end of the absoluteness of metaphysics. Accepting the constitutively divided, unstable, and plural condition that belongs to our own Being, destined to difference, to impermanency, and to multiplicity, means being able to actively practice solidarity, charity, and irony. The man who withdraws his attention from the supernatural world and concentrates on this world and this time ("*saeculum*" means also "this present time") exerts himself to realize the ideals of pluralism and tolerance and to prevent any particular vision of the world from imposing itself by means of the authority attributed to it. The "death of God" (an expression that originally belonged to Luther) today refers to the incarnation, the *kenosis* (from the verb "*kenóo* [I empty]") with which Paul alludes to the "emptying out of itself" accomplished by the divine *verbum* that has lowered itself to the human condition in order to die on the cross. All this propels us toward a less objective and more interpretive conception of the revelation, which is to say, toward a conception of the weakness proper to "the last God."

Today we can no longer think of God as the motionless foundation of history because the truth of such a God is no longer among the goals of knowledge: in place of the search for truth, we seek solidarity, charity, and irony. Thought must abandon all objective, universal, and apodictic foundational claims in order to prevent Christianity, allied with metaphysics in the search for first principles, from making room for violence. Hermeneutics has been the friendliest philosophy toward religion because of its critique of the idea of truth as conformity between propositions and objects. From the point of view of the return of religiosity, the prominence of hermeneutics in contemporary culture seems to indicate, much more than in any previous epoch, that the road to salvation does not pass through description and knowledge but through interpretation and edification. The role that notions such as "communication," "globalization," "dialogue," "consensus," "interpretation," "democracy," and "charity" have gained in our contemporary culture is not casual but indicates a movement of modern thought toward conceiving of truth more as charity than as objectivity.[13]

Weak thought looks for compatibility only with religious faith that is trying to "privatize" itself, not with religious faiths that found churches and adopt political positions. If laicism amounts to no more than anticlericalism, in other words the tendency to affirm the complete autonomy of cultural, social, and political life from any church, then the future of religion, according to Rorty and Vattimo, will depend on the ability of today's ecclesiastical authorities to allow religion to transform itself into something private.[14] The problem of sin also ceases to be something public, something so oppressive as to drive certain individuals to suicide. If religion were to succeed definitively in becoming a private question in today's age of interpretation, linked solely to individual capacities, then postmodern man would become an agent responsible no longer to God but to himself and others. Democracy, hermeneutics, and Christianity, from a postmetaphysical point of view, are not methods of discovering truth, and they deliberately bracket all questions regarding truth. Whatever future awaits us will depend on the capacity of culture to annul all the reasons for conflict and to assume the program of secularization as its task. Thanks to this program, it is much more difficult today to resort to religion in order to legitimize political positions or "just" wars.[15] It may indeed be the case that the preferred philosopher of President George W. Bush is Jesus Christ, but it is far from likely that the preferred president of Jesus Christ is a politician who improperly enlists him as an ally in wars against the fundamentalists of other religions.

The truth that shall make us free (John 8.32) is not the objective truth of theology and the natural sciences: the scriptural revelation contains no explanation of how God is made or how to save ourselves through knowledge of the truth. The only truth that the Bible reveals to us is the practical appeal to love, to charity. The truth of Christianity is the dissolution of the metaphysical concept of truth itself. Christianity without God represents a faith free from the objectivistic metaphysics that believed in its own ability to demonstrate, on the basis of "sound natural reason," the existence of a Supreme Being. The main challenge undertaken by the Catholic Church in modernity was the same as the one undertaken by science: both wished to prevail as the only source of truth. Debates concerning the proofs of the existence of God, or of miracles, always turned on the idea that the truth that will set us free is the objective truth.

The disputes on the problems of bioethics and on the significance of sexuality constitute the terrain on which, at present, the Church's claim to speak in the name of humanity and not of a positive revelation is most strongly asserted. But the problem of the relationship to science is not the only one: the demands for emancipation of vast sectors of the faithful also constitute a problem that the pope does not address on historical grounds. The refusal of women's priesthood, for example, is motivated by the loyalty of the church to a "natural" vocation of woman that can only be taken seriously within a metaphysical, rigid, and medieval frame of reference. In the postmodern condition it is precisely this doctrinal, moral, and disciplinary function that Christianity can no longer carry out; the most it can hope for is to participate in the confrontation between cultures and religions by insisting on its own specific orientation to laicity. This orientation already manifested itself, in contrast to other religions, in the strong missionary component of early Christianity, when the apostles were sent to preach the gospel to all communities; then, during the terrible wars of religion in Europe, Christian universalism discovered the idea of tolerance, of laicity. These profound historical experiences still emerge in phenomena such as Christmas or the cross, which have become holidays and signs for everyone, even those who do not believe. From this perspective, the pope has no good reason to complain that Christmas has become too laic and worldly a holiday or that the cross has become an ornament that no longer represents an affirmation of Christian identity.

The fact that today most practicing Catholics find their own sexual ethics contrary to the ones preached by the Church amounts to an appeal for the privatization of religion. If the church continues to present itself with the force of authority, it risks marginality and indirectly obliges its own believers to privatize their faith. Today, there are few Catholics who do not favor freedom of decision regarding birth control, the marriage of priests, the ordination of women, the free election of bishops by priests, the use of condoms as a precaution against AIDS, the admission to communion of divorcees who remarry, the legalization of abortion; above all, there are few who do not believe that it is possible to be a good Catholic and publicly disagree with the teachings of the Church. If the Catholic Church is to have a future as an institution in the twenty-first century, it will require a papacy that is not above the world, as the head of the Church, but in the Church as, in the words of Pope Gregory the Great, the "servant of the servants of God." The Catholic Church no longer needs primacy in law and honor; it needs a constructive pastoral primacy, in the sense of a spiritual guide, concentrating on the duties required by the present. It should no longer be a patriarchal Eurocentric church, but a universal and tolerant one, guarantor of the autonomy of national, regional, and local churches—as Hans Küng several times suggests. An immeasurable number of Christians, in communities and groups throughout the whole world, are living out an authentic ecumenism centered on the gospel regardless of any resistance by the ecclesiastical hierarchy: the challenge of the future will be to convince the Church that charity must take the place of discipline. Yet while all these believers are participating fully in the life of their own postmodern times and consider the Hebrew-Christian revelation as an appeal for a dialogic culture, the pope and his bishops tend to remain entrenched in authoritarian positions.[16]

The texts and the dialogue that compose this book sketch out the map of a faith without precepts and, most of all, without the image of a metaphysical God. Rorty's text, "Anticlericalism and Atheism," explains how, with the end of metaphysics, being religious no longer means dependence upon

specifically observable phenomena regarded as intuitively evident. Commenting in detail upon Vattimo's book *Belief,* Rorty
observes that objective metaphysics has dissolved along with
thought that identified the truth of being with the manipula-
bility of the objects of science; the way for an anti-essentialist
religion was thus finally opened. This religion, grounded
exclusively on private motivation, is destined to realize the
promise of the gospel that from now on God regards us not as
servants but as friends. Rorty, who calls himself a "laic anti-
clerical" points out that we cannot try to legitimize these postmodern interpretations of Christianity because the concept of
"legitimacy" is not applicable to what each of us does in his
own solitude. Vattimo's text, "The Age of Interpretation,"
starts by showing how hermeneutics has changed the reality of
things, historicizing philosophy and putting the distinction
between natural and human sciences completely out of
bounds. Hermeneutics becomes the very enunciation of historical existence in the age of the end of metaphysics, since it
affirms that the thesis that "there are no facts, only interpretations" is in turn an interpretation. According to Vattimo, this
recognition has come about thanks in part to Christianity,
which introduced into the world the principle of interiority,
dissolving the experience of objective reality into one of "listening to and interpreting messages"; this hermeneuticization
of philosophy freed religion from metaphysics at the moment
when it had identified the death of God, announced by Nietzsche, with the death of Christ on the cross narrated by the
Gospels. If today we still believe in the salvific significance of
this death, it is because we have read it in the Gospels, certainly not because we have objective proofs of the historical
fact of the resurrection. Invoking Croce, Vattimo concludes by
observing that the antifoundational pragmatism of Rorty is
itself only possible because we live in a society that has its roots
in the biblical message. Pragmatism and hermeneutics have

become philosophies capable of going beyond the metaphysical Logos, toward a culture of dialogue no longer driven by the search for truth. Finally, in the dialogue, "What is Religion's future after Metaphysics?" the future of religion is analyzed together with the political, social, and historical aspects that characterize our postmodern society, in the hope that one day solidarity, charity, and irony will become the only law.

Notes

1. R. Rorty, "Being That Can Be Understood Is Language," *London Review of Books* 22, no. 6 (16 March 2000): 25. By the German term "*Überwindung*," we should understand the "overcoming" of metaphysics; and by "*Verwindung*," the "turning to new purposes," as Rorty rightly says, or even the "surpassing," "twisting," "resigning ourselves to," and "ironic acceptance of" metaphysics.

2. G. Vattimo, "Gadamer and the Problem of Ontology," in *Gadamer's Century: Essays in Honor of Hans-Georg Gadamer*, ed. J. Malpas, U. Arnswald, and J. Kertscher, (Cambridge, Mass.: The MIT Press, 2002), 305–6. Rorty and Vattimo think that hermeneutics prevents the space left open by the end of metaphysics from being filled up by another foundational philosophy and, above all, that the goal of philosophical research is no longer contact with something that exists independently from us, but only the formation of ourselves, *Bildung*. For an accurate analysis of the meaning of hermeneutics for philosophy, see R. Rorty, *Philosophy and the Mirror of Nature* (Princeton, N.J: Princeton University Press, 1979); and G. Vattimo, *Beyond Interpretation: The Meaning of Hermeneutics for Philosophy*, trans. David Webb (Cambridge: Polity Press, 1997).

3. Rorty believes we must insist on this analogy between theological and philosophical convictions because he sees

> the Western Rationalistic Tradition as a secularized version of the Western Monotheist Tradition—as the latest twist on what Heidegger calls "onto-theology." We pragmatists take the same dim view of Absolute Truth and of Reality as It Is in Itself as the Enlightenment took of Divine Wrath and Divine Judgment. . . . Dewey was happy to

admit that these distinctions had, in their time, served us well. In their time, they were neither confusions nor repressive devices nor mystifications. On the contrary, they were instruments that Greek thinkers used to change social conditions, often for the better. But over a couple of millennia, these instruments outlived their usefulness. Dewey thought that, just as many Christians had outgrown the need to ask whether the sentences of the Creed correspond to objective reality, so civilization as a whole might outgrow the supposed necessity to believe in absolute truths. Dewey learned from Hegel to historicize everything, including Hegel's own picturesque but outdated story of the union of subject and object at the end of History. Like Marx, Dewey dropped Hegel's notion of Absolute Spirit, but kept his insight that ideas and movements that had begun as instruments of emancipation (Greek metaphysics, Christianity, the rise of the bourgeoisie, the Hegelian System) had typically, over the course of time, turned into instruments of repression—into parts of what Dewey called "the crust of convention."

R. Rorty, *Truth and Progress*
(Cambridge: Cambridge University Press, 1998), 76–78.

4. When metaphysics cannot be overcome, *überwunden*, but only surpassed, "accepted ironically," or *verwunden*, philosophy becomes "weak thought," the weakening of the terminologies that still refer to objects. Vattimo specifies that "weak thought" is not simply

the idea of a thinking that is more aware of its own limits, that abandons its claims to global and metaphysical visions, but above all a theory of weakening as the constitutive character of Being in the epoch of the end of metaphysics. If, indeed, Heidegger's critique of objectivistic metaphysics cannot be carried forward by replacing the latter with a more adequate conception of Being (still thought of as an object), one will have to think Being as not identified, in any sense, with the presence characteristic of the object.

G. Vattimo, *Belief*, trans. Luca D'Isanto and David Webb
(Stanford, Calif.: Stanford University Press, 1999), 35.

Rorty not only says that his essays "should be read as examples of what a group of contemporary Italian philosophers have called 'weak thought'—philosophical reflection which does not attempt a radical criticism of contemporary culture, does not attempt to refound or remotivate it, but simply assembles reminders and suggests some interesting possibilities" (R. Rorty, *Essays on Heidegger and Others* [Cambridge: Cambridge University Press, 1991], 6), but also that

> we will always be held captive by some picture or other, for this is merely to say we shall never escape from language or from metaphor—never see either God or the Intrinsic Nature of Reality face to face. But old pictures may have disadvantages that can be avoided by the sketching of new pictures. Escape from prejudice and superstition, Dewey thought, was not escape from appearance to reality, but escape from the satisfaction of old needs to the satisfaction of new needs. It was a process of maturation, not progress from darkness to light. On this view, escape from the Western Rationalistic Tradition would indeed be an escape from error to truth, but it would not be an escape from the way things appear to the way things really are.
>
> Rorty, *Truth and Progress*, 80.

5. This is indeed the fundamental problem of philosophy today: taking leave of the foundational illusion, can philosophy really continue without ontological prejudices? On one side, Vattimo explains that we

> know that some interpreters and radical continuators of Heidegger, Jacques Derrida in the lead, deny that it is still possible to speak of Being because this would be a sort of lapse back into the metaphysics of foundations. Yet to continue to speak of Being and ontology is not an excessive claim; it is rather an expression of modesty on the part of this philosophy, which knows that it is not obliged to respond to truth but only to the need to recompose the experience of a historical phase of humanity that is living through the fragmentation of the division of labor, the compartmentalization of language, the many forms of discontinuity to which we are exposed by the rapidity of the

transformation (technological above all) of our world. On the contrary, you can only set Being to one side if you neglect this modest task and suppose that you must in any case still answer to an objective truth of things, which would exclude just such a "simulation" as being too vague and too rigid at the same time.

Defined as the ontology of actuality, philosophy is practiced as an interpretation of the epoch, a giving-form to widely felt sentiments about the meaning of being alive in a certain society and in a certain historical world. I am well aware that defining philosophy as the Hegelian spirit of the age is like reinventing the wheel. The difference, though, lies in the "interpretation": philosophy is not the expression of the age, it is interpretation, and although it does strive to be persuasive, it also acknowledges its own contingency, liberty, perilousness. It is not just Hegel who seems to be returning; empiricism is playing a part as well. The epoch and the widespread sense of what it means are perhaps no more than experience, to which empiricists once sought to remain true—experience interpreted philosophically, meaning in continuity with and employing the same instruments as a certain textual tradition. Within this tradition certain elements, aspects, and authors are of course privileged over others, but it remains present in its totality as background, as a possible source of alternative interpretations.

> G. Vattimo, *Nihilism and Emancipation:*
> *Ethics, Politics, and Law,*
> ed. Santiago Zabala, trans. W. McCuaig (New York:
> Columbia University Press, 2004), chapter 7.

On the other hand, Rorty says that

the point is that some of us (not everybody) cannot circumvent the metaphysical *logos* without mutilating ourselves, without curtailing our knowledge of what made us what we are (including the mutilations that made us what we are), and thus our knowledge of what we are. If so, the point is not that there is an exceptionally adhesive substance called "philosophy" (one whose properties are

understood by Derrida but not by his nominalistic com-
petitors in the antimetaphysics business), but rather that
Derrida and Bennington are, following Heidegger, using
"philosophy" as a name for the sequence of "words of
Being"—the words that, had they not been uttered, would
have resulted in our being different people. Some people
may not be able to walk away from the metaphysical *logos*
or from the Greek-Jew contrast without losing their sense
of where they are. That was why Heidegger insisted that
denken ist andenken, and it may be why Derrida and Bennington view nominalistic pragmatists like me as light-
minded escapists.

> Rorty, *Truth and Progress,* 343–44.

6. Rorty explains that it was Hegel who first criticized his predecessors not because their propositions were false but because their language was obsolete, and he "broke away from the Plato-Kant sequence
and began a tradition of ironist philosophy which is continued in Nietzsche, Heidegger, and Derrida. These are the philosophers who define
their achievement by their relation to their predecessors rather than by
their relation to the truth." R. Rorty, *Contingency, Irony, and Solidarity*
(Cambridge: Cambridge University Press, 1989), 79. He also maintains
that no

matter what one's opinion of the secularization of culture,
it was a mistake to try to make the natural scientist into a
new sort of priest, a link between the human and the non-
human. So was the idea that some sorts of truths are
"objective" whereas others are merely "subjective" or "relative"—the attempt to divide up the set of true sentences
into "genuine knowledge" and "mere opinion," or into
the "factual" and "judgmental." So was the idea that the
scientist has a special method which, if only the humanist
would apply it to ultimate values, would give us the same
kind of self-confidence about moral ends as we now have
about technological means. I think that we should content
ourselves with the second, "weaker" conception of rationality, and avoid the first, "stronger" conception.

> R. Rorty, *Objectivism, Relativism, and Truth*
> (Cambridge: Cambridge University Press, 1991), 37.

7. "For example," Vattimo explains,

one might ask how we can rationally argue once we forgo the claim of grasping an ultimate foundation that would be valid for all, above and beyond any cultural difference. To this one might answer: the universal validity of an assertion can be constructed by building consensus in dialogue, though without claiming any right in the name of an absolute truth. Dialogical consensus may be reached by acknowledging that we share a heritage of cultural, historical, and technological-scientific acquisitions.

G. Vattimo, After Christianity, trans. L. D'Isanto
(New York: Columbia University Press, 2002), 5.

8. John Paul II, *Fides et ratio* (encyclical letter), 15 September 1998, §5.

9. See Thomas Kuhn, *The Structure of Scientific Revolutions*, 3rd ed. (Chicago: University of Chicago Press, 1996); Arthur Fine, *The Shaky Game: Einstein, Realism, and the Quantum Theory* (Chicago: University of Chicago Press, 1996); Robert Brandom, *Making it Explicit: Reasoning, Representing, and Discursive Commitment*, (Cambridge, Mass.: Harvard University Press, 1994); Bas van Fraassen, *The Empirical Stance*, (New Haven, Conn.: Yale University Press, 2002); Jack Miles, *Christ: A Crisis in the Life of God* (New York: Alfred A Knopf, 2001); and Carmelo Dotolo, *La rivelazione cristiana: Parola, evento, mistero* (Milan: Paoline, 2002). On the return of religion in the third century see Jacques Derrida and Gianni Vattimo, eds., *Religion*, trans. David Webb and others (Stanford, Calif.: Stanford University Press, 1998); Nancy K. Frankenberry, ed., *Radical Interpretation in Religion* (Cambridge: Cambridge University Press, 2002); and Mark Wrathall, ed., *Religion after Metaphysics* (Cambridge: Cambridge University Press, 2003).

10. Vattimo specifies that "philosophy can call the weakening that it discovers as the characteristic feature of the history of Being secularization in its broadest sense, which comprises all the forms of dissolution of the sacred characteristic of the modern process of civilization. If it is the mode in which the weakening of Being realizes itself as the *kenosis* of God, which is the kernel of the history of salvation, secularization shall no longer be conceived of as abandonment of religion but as the paradoxical realization of Being's religious vocation." Vattimo, *After Christianity*, 24.

11. Many philosophers and also a large number of contemporary scientists and theologians are mostly irreligious or antireligious through mere inertia, not for theoretical reasons. According to Vattimo, if

> god is dead, if philosophy has recognized that it cannot with certainty grasp the ultimate foundation, then philosophical atheism is no longer necessary. Only an absolute philosophy can feel the necessity of refuting religious experience. . . . Nietzsche writes that God is dead because those who believe in him have killed him. In other words, the faithful, who have learned not to lie because it was God's command, have discovered in the end that God himself is a superfluous lie. However, in light of our postmodern experience, this means: since God can no longer be upheld as an ultimate foundation, as the absolute metaphysical structure of the real, it is possible, once again, to believe in God. True, it is not the God of metaphysics or of medieval scholasticism. But that is not the God of the Bible, of the Book that was dissolved and dismissed by modern rationalist and absolutist metaphysics.
>
> Vattimo, *After Christianity*, 5–6.

12. On this matter see R. Rorty, "Ethics Without Principles," in his *Philosophy and Social Hope* (London: Penguin, 1999), 72–90; and G. Vattimo, "Ethics Without Transcendence?" in his *Nihilism and Emancipation*, ed. Santiago Zabala, trans. W. McCuaig (New York: Columbia University Press, in press).

13. For an accurate analysis of religion in Rorty and Vattimo, see the major studies by D. Vaden House, *Without God or His Doubles: Realism, Relativism, and Rorty* (Leiden, the Netherlands: E. J. Brill, 1994); and Carmelo Dotolo, *La teologia fondamentale davanti alle sfide del "pensiero debole" di G. Vattimo* (Rome: LAS, 1999).

14. This, originally, was the opinion of Thomas Jefferson, who set the tone for American liberal politics when he said "it does me no injury for my neighbor to say that there are twenty Gods or no God." "His example," Rorty explains,

> helped make respectable the idea that politics can be separated from beliefs about matters of ultimate importance—that shared belief among citizens on such matters

are not essential to a democratic society. Like many other figures of the Enlightenment, Jefferson assumed that a moral faculty common to the typical theist and the typical atheist suffices for civic virtue. . . . He thought it enough to privatize religion, to view it as irrelevant to social order but relevant to, and possibly essential for, individual perfection. Citizens of a Jeffersonian democracy can be as religious or irreligious as they please as long as they are not "fanatical." That is, they must abandon or modify opinions on matters of ultimate importance, the opinions that may hitherto have given sense and point to their lives, if these opinions entail public actions that cannot be justified to most of their fellow citizens.

Rorty, *Objectivism, Relativism, and Truth,* 175.

15. "Thanks to the secularizing influences of the recent West," Rorty says,

it has become increasingly difficult to use religion to sanctify oppression. (This seems to me one almost *entirely* good thing which Westernization has done for the East, though I admit that the Western colonialists tried to use Christianity to legitimize their own oppression when they first arrived.) It has become increasingly easier for the weak and the poor to see themselves as victims of the greed of their fellow-humans rather than of Destiny, or the gods, or of the sins of their ancestors.

R. Rorty, quoted in Balslev Anindita Niyogi,
Cultural Otherness: Correspondence with Richard Rorty
(New Delhi: Indian Institute of
Advanced Study, 1991), 100.

Vattimo too suggests that

what, from a Christian point of view, and in general from a "Western" point of view, one can and should do in order to escape from the miscomprehensions of the wars of religion, is to start to live our own religiosity outside the schema dear to rationalistic illuminism which foresees only two possibilities: either the fanaticism of blind faith (*credo quia absurdum*), or the skepticism of a reason without roots and without an effective grip on the world. Concretely, an attitude of recovered religiosity free from power concerns, therefore also free from any temptation of violent imposition, would mean that today's West, instead of preparing for an endless war for the triumph of its own "faith," should take seriously the historical reasons for its clashes with the so-called third world. These are mainly reasons of economics, of inequality, of exploitation, disguising themselves as reasons of faith and of culture exclusively in aid of self-interested ideological manipulation by those who hold wealth and power. May we hope to find in the other interlocutors in our dialogue, especially our Muslim and Hebrew friends, the same spirit? Rather than seeking the triumph of one faith over the others, the task facing us all is to rediscover—after the "metaphysical" age of absolutisms and of the identity between truth and authority—the possibility of a post-modern religious experience in which the relation with the divine is no longer corrupted by fear, violence, and superstition.

G. Vattimo, *Vero e falso Universalismo cristiano*
(Rio de Janerio: Editora Universitária Candido Mendes,
Academia da Latinidade, 2002), 16.

16. This point regarding the "sexual ethics of the Church" is analyzed and discussed in the dialogue of this book. Rorty has specified recently that

religion is less important now than 100 years ago. The tide of faith has ebbed. Lots of people are commonsensically secular in a way that their ancestors couldn't have been commonsensically secular. I certainly don't think we have to get back to Christianity, or Marxism, or any other absolutist view in order to get anything political done. . . . [And] like the priests, they like to think they have a privileged relation to reality. I doubt they do, but one might expect that they would resent it if told they don't. When the priests of the 19th century were told by practitioners of philological higher criticism of the Bible that they were in the service of middle-eastern creation myths, they didn't like it. In the middle of this century, the physicists didn't like it when Kuhn told them they were just trying to solve puzzles.

Richard Rorty, in R. Rorty, D. Nystrom, K. Puckett,
Against Bosses, Against Oligarchies:
A Conversation with Richard Rorty
(Chicago: Prickly Paradigm Press, 2002), 59–61.

1

Anticlericalism and Atheism

Richard Rorty

SOME DAY, INTELLECTUAL historians may remark that the twentieth century was the one in which the philosophy professors began to stop asking bad questions—questions like "What really exists?" "What are the scope and limits of human knowledge?" and "How does language hook up with reality?" These questions assume that philosophy can be done ahistorically. They presuppose the bad idea that inspection of our present practices can give us an understanding of the "structure" of all possible human practices.

"Structure" is just another word for "essence." The most important movements in twentieth-century philosophy have been anti-essentialist. These movements have mocked the ambitions of their predecessors, positivism and phenomenology, to do what Plato and Aristotle had hoped to do—sift out the changing appearances from the enduringly real, the merely contingent from the truly necessary. Recent examples of this mockery are Jacques Derrida's *Margins of Philosophy* and Bas van Fraassen's *The Empirical Stance*. These books stand on the shoulders of Heidegger's *Being and Time*, Dewey's *Reconstruction in Philosophy*, and Wittgenstein's *Philosophical Investigations*. All these anti-essentialist books urge us to fight free of the old Greek distinctions between the apparent and the real and between the necessary and the contingent.

One effect of the rise of anti-essentialism and of historicism is insouciance about what Lecky famously called "the warfare between science and theology." A growing tendency to accept what Terry Pinkard calls "Hegel's doctrine of the sociality of reason" and to abandon what Habermas calls "subject-centered reason" for what he calls "communicative reason" has weakened the grip of the idea that scientific beliefs are formed rationally, whereas religious beliefs are not. The antipositivist tenor of post-Kuhnian philosophy of science has combined with the work of post-Heideggerian theologians to make intellectuals more sympathetic to William James's claim that natural science and religion need not compete with one another.

These developments have made the word "atheist" less popular than it used to be. Philosophers who do not go to church are now less inclined to describe themselves as believing that there is no God. They are more inclined to use such expressions as Max Weber's "religiously unmusical." One can be tone-deaf when it comes to religion just as one can be oblivious to the charms of music. People who find themselves quite unable to take an interest in the question of whether God exists have no right to be contemptuous of people who believe passionately in his existence or of people who deny it with equal passion. Nor do either of the latter have a right to be contemptuous of those to whom the dispute seems pointless.

Philosophy resembles music and religion in this respect. Many students—those who walk out of the final examination in Philosophy 101 determined never to waste their time with another philosophy course and unable to understand how people can take that sort of thing seriously—are philosophically unmusical. Some philosophers still think that this attitude toward the discipline to which they have devoted their lives is evidence of an intellectual, and perhaps even a moral flaw. But most are by now content to shrug off an inability to take philosophical issues seriously as no more important, when evaluating a person's intellect or character, than an inability to read fiction or to grasp mathematical relationships or to learn foreign languages.

This increased tolerance for people who simply brush aside questions that were once thought to be of the highest importance is sometimes described as the adoption of an "aestheticist" attitude. This description is especially popular among those who find such tolerance deplorable and who diagnose its spread as a symptom of a dangerous spiritual illness ("skepticism" or "relativism" or something equally appalling). But the term "aesthetic" in such contexts presupposes the standard Kantian cognitive-moral-aesthetic distinction. That distinction is itself one of the principal targets of anti-essentialist, historicist philosophizing.

Kantians think that once you have given up hope of attaining universal agreement on an issue you have declared it "merely a matter of taste." But this description strikes anti-essentialist philosophers as just as bad as the Kantian idea that being rational is a matter of following rules. Philosophers who do not believe that there are any such rules reject Kantian pigeonholing in favor of questions about what context certain beliefs or practices or books can best be put in, for what particular purposes. Once the Kantian trichtomy is abandoned, the work of theologians like Bultmann and Tillich no longer looks like a reduction of the "cognitive" claims of religion to "merely" aesthetic claims.

In this new climate of philosophical opinion, philosophy professors are no longer expected to provide answers to a question that exercised both Kant and Hegel: How can the worldview of natural science be fitted together with the complex of religious and moral ideas that were central to European civilization? We know what it is like to fit physics together with chemistry and chemistry together with biology, but that sort of fitting is inappropriate when thinking about the interface between art and morality or between politics and jurisprudence or between religion and natural science. All these spheres of culture continually interpenetrate and interact. There is no need for an organizational chart that specifies, once and for all, when they are permitted to do so. Nor is there any need to attempt to reach an ahistorical, God's-eye overview of the relations between all human practices. We can settle for the more limited task Hegel called "holding our time in thought."

Given all these changes, it is not surprising that only two sorts of philosophers are still tempted to use the word "atheist" to describe themselves. The first sort are those who still think that belief in the divine is an empirical hypothesis and that modern science has given better explanations of the phenomena God was once used to explain. Philosophers of this sort are delighted whenever an ingenuous natural scientist claims that some new scientific discovery provides evidence for the truth of theism, for they find it easy to debunk this claim. They can do so simply by trotting out the same sorts of arguments about the irrelevance of any particular empirical state of affairs to the existence of an atemporal and nonspatial being as were used by Hume and Kant against the natural theologians of the eighteenth century.

I agree with Hume and Kant that the notion of "empirical evidence" is irrelevant to talk about God,[1] but this point bears equally against atheism and theism. President Bush made a good point when he said, in a speech designed to please Christian fundamentalists, that "atheism is a faith" because it is "subject to neither confirmation nor refutation by means of argument or evidence." But the same goes, of course, for theism. Neither those who affirm nor those who deny the existence of God can plausibly claim that they have evidence for their views. Being religious, in the modern West, does not have much to do with the explanation of specific observable phenomena.

But there is a second sort of philosopher who describes himself or herself as an atheist. These are the ones who use "atheism" as a rough synonym for "anticlericalism." I now wish that I had used the latter term on the occasions when I have used the former to characterize my own view. For anticlericalism is a political view, not an epistemological or metaphysical one. It is the view that ecclesiastical institutions, despite all the good they do—despite all the comfort they provide to those in need or in despair—are dangerous to the health of democratic societies.[2] Whereas the philosophers who claim that atheism, unlike theism, is backed up by evidence would say that religious belief is irrational, contemporary secularists like myself are content to say that it is politically dangerous. On our view, religion is unobjectionable as long as it is privatized—as long as ecclesiastical institutions do not attempt to rally the faithful behind political proposals and as long as believers and unbelievers agree to follow a policy of live and let live.

Some of those who hold this view, such as myself, had no religious upbringing and have never developed any attachment to any religious tradition. We are the ones who call ourselves "religiously unmusical." But others, such as the distinguished contemporary Italian philosopher Gianni Vattimo, have used their philosophical learning and sophistication to argue for the reasonableness of a return to the religiosity of their youth. This argument is laid out in Vattimo's moving and original book *Credere di credere*.[3] His response to the question "Do you now once again believe in God?" amounts to saying: I find myself becoming more and more religious, so I suppose I must believe in God. But I think Vattimo might have done better to say: I am becoming more and more religious, and so coming to have what many people would call a belief in God, but I am not sure that the term "belief" is the right description of what I have.

The point of such a reformulation would be to take account of our conviction that if a belief is true, everybody ought to share it. But Vattimo does not think that all human beings ought to be theists, much less that they should all be Catholics. He follows William James in disassociating the question "Have I a right to be religious?" from the question "Should everybody believe in the existence of God?" Just insofar as one accepts the familiar Hume/Kant critique of natural theology but disagrees with the positivistic claim that the explanatory successes of modern science have rendered belief in God irrational, one will be inclined to say that religiosity is not happily characterized by the term "belief." So one should welcome Vattimo's attempt to move religion out of the epistemic arena, an arena in which it seems subject to challenge by natural science.

Such attempts are, of course, not new. Kant's suggestion that we view God as a postulate of pure practical reason rather than an explanation of empirical phenomena cleared the way for thinkers like Schleiermacher to develop what Nancy Frankenberry has called "a theology of symbolic forms." It also encouraged thinkers like Kierkegaard, Barth, and Lévinas to make God wholly other—beyond the reach not only of evidence and argument but of discursive thought.

Vattimo's importance lies in his rejection of both of these unhappy post-Kantian initiatives. He puts aside the attempt to connect religion with truth and so has no use for notions like "symbolic" or "emotional" or "metaphorical" or "moral" truth. Nor does he have any use for what he calls (somewhat misleadingly, in my opinion) "existentialist theology"—the attempt to make religiosity a matter of being rescued from sin by the inexplicable grace of a deity wholly other than man. His theology is explicitly designed for those whom he calls "half-believers," the people whom St. Paul called "lukewarm in the faith"—the sort of people who only go to church for weddings, baptisms, and funerals (69).

Vattimo turns away from the passages in Epistle to the Romans that Karl Barth liked best, and reduces the Christian message to the passage in Paul that most other people like best: 1 Corinthians 13. His strategy is to treat the Incarnation as God's sacrifice of all his power and authority, as well as all his otherness. The Incarnation was an act of *kenosis*, the act in which God turned everything over to human beings. This enables Vattimo to make his most startling and most important claim: that "secularization . . . is the constitutive trait of authentic religious experience" (21).

Hegel too saw human history as constituting the Incarnation of the Spirit, and its slaughter-bench as the cross. But Hegel was unwilling to put aside truth in favor of love. So Hegel turns human history into a dramatic narrative that reaches its climax in an epistemic state: absolute knowledge. For Vattimo, by contrast, there is no internal dynamic, no inherent teleology to human history; there is no great drama to be unfolded, but only the hope that love may prevail. Vattimo thinks that if we take human history as seriously as Hegel did, while refusing to place it within either an epistemological or a metaphysical context, we can stop the pendulum from swinging back and forth between militantly positivistic atheism and symbolist or existentialist defenses of theism. As he says, "It is (only) because metaphysical meta-narratives have been dissolved that philosophy has rediscovered the plausibility of religion and can consequently approach the religious need of common consciousness independently of the framework of Enlightenment critique."[4] Vattimo wants to dissolve the problem of the coexistence of natural science with the legacy of Christianity by identifying Christ neither with truth nor with power but with love alone.

Vattimo's argument provides an illustration of how lines of thought drawn from Nietzsche and Heidegger can be intertwined with those drawn from James and Dewey. For these two intellectual traditions have in common the thought that the quest for truth and knowledge is no more and no less than the quest for intersubjective agreement. The epistemic arena is a public space, a space from which religion can and should retreat.[5] The realization that it should retreat from that sphere is not a recognition of the true essence of religion, but simply one of the morals to be drawn from the history of Europe and America.

Vattimo says that "now that Cartesian (and Hegelian) thought has completed its parabola, it no longer makes sense to oppose faith and reason so sharply" (Vattimo, *Belief*, 87). By Cartesian and Hegelian thought, Vattimo means pretty much what Heidegger meant by "onto-theology." The term covers not only traditional theology and metaphysics but also positivism and (insofar as it is an attempt to put philosophy on the secure path of a science) phenomenology. He agrees with Heidegger that "the metaphysics of objectivity culminates in a thinking that identifies the truth of Being with the calculable, measurable and definitively manipulatable object of techno-science" (30). For if you identify rationality with the pursuit of universal intersubjective agreement and truth with the outcome of such a pursuit, and if you also claim that nothing should take precedence over that pursuit, then you will squeeze religion not only out of public life but out of intellectual life. This is because you will have made natural science the paradigm of rationality and truth. Then religion will have to be thought of either as an unsuccessful competitor with empirical inquiry or as "merely" a vehicle of emotional satisfaction.

To save religion from onto-theology, you need to regard the desire for universal intersubjective agreement as just one human need among many others, and one that does not automatically trump all other needs. This is a doctrine Nietzsche and Heidegger share with James and Dewey. All four of these anti-Cartesians have principled objections to the pejorative use of "merely" in expressions such as "merely private" or "merely literary" or "merely aesthetic" or "merely emotional." They all provide reasons both for replacing the Kantian distinction between the cognitive and the noncognitive with the distinction between the satisfaction of public needs and the satisfaction of private needs, and for insisting that there is nothing "mere" about satisfaction of the latter. All four are, in the words that Vattimo uses to describe Heidegger, trying to help us "quit a horizon of thought that is an enemy of freedom and of the historicity of existing" (31).

If one stays within this horizon of thought and so continues to think of epistemology and metaphysics as first philosophy, one will be convinced that all one's assertions should have cognitive content. An assertion has such content insofar as it is caught up in what the contemporary American philosopher Robert Brandom calls "the game of giving and asking for reasons." But to say that religion should be privatized is to say that religious people are entitled, for certain purposes, to opt out of this game. They are entitled to disconnect their assertions from the network of socially acceptable inferences that provide justifications for making these assertions and draw practical consequences from having made them.

Vattimo seems to be aiming at such a privatized religion when he describes the secularization of European culture as the fulfillment of the promise of the Incarnation, considered as *kenosis*, God's turning everything over to us. The more secular, the less hierocratic the West becomes, the better it carries out the Gospels' promise that God will no longer see us as servants but as friends. "The essence of the [Christian] revelation," Vattimo says, "is reduced to charity, while all the rest is left to the non-finality of diverse historical experiences" (77).

This account of the essence of Christianity—one in which God's self-emptying and man's attempt to think of love as the only law are two faces of the same coin—permits Vattimo to see all the great unmaskers of the West, from Copernicus and Newton to Darwin, Nietzsche, and Freud, as carrying out works of love. These men were, in his words, "reading the signs of the times with no other provision than that of the commandment of love" (66). They were followers of Christ in the sense that "Christ himself is the unmasker, and . . . the unmasking inaugurated by him . . . is the meaning of the history of salvation itself" (66).

To ask whether this is a "legitimate" or "valid" version of Catholicism, or of Christianity, would be to pose exactly the wrong question. The notion of "legitimacy" is not applicable to what Vattimo, or any of the rest of us, does with our solitude. To try to apply it is to imply that you have no right to go to church for the weddings and baptisms and funerals of your friends and relations unless you acknowledge the authority of ecclesiastical institutions to decide who counts as a Christian and who does not, or no right to call yourself a Jew unless you perform this ritual rather than that.

I can summarize the line of thought that Vattimo and I are pursuing as follows: The battle between religion and science conducted in the eighteenth and nineteenth centuries was a contest between institutions, both of which claimed cultural supremacy. It was a good thing for both religion and science that science won that battle. For truth and knowledge are a matter of social cooperation, and science gives us the means to carry out better cooperative social projects than before. If social cooperation is what you want, the conjunction of the science and the common sense of your day is all you need. But if you want something else, then a religion that has been taken out of the epistemic arena, a religion that finds the question of theism versus atheism uninteresting, may be just what suits your solitude.

It may be, but it may not. There is still a big difference between people like myself and people like Vattimo. Considering that he was raised a Catholic and I was raised in no religion at all, this is not surprising. Only if one thinks that religious yearnings are somehow precultural and "basic to human nature" will one be reluctant to leave the matter at that—reluctant to privatize religion completely by letting it swing free of the demand for universality.

But if one gives up the idea that either the quest for truth or the quest for God is hard-wired into all human organisms and allows that both are matters of cultural formation, then such privatization will seem natural and proper. People like Vattimo will cease to think that my lack of religious feeling is a sign of vulgarity, and people like me will cease to think that his possession of such feelings is a sign of cowardice. Both of us can cite 1 Corinthians 13 in support of our refusal to engage in any such invidious explanations.

My differences with Vattimo come down to his ability to regard a past event as holy and my sense that holiness resides only in an ideal future. Vattimo thinks of God's decision to switch from being our master to being our friend as the decisive event upon which our present efforts are dependent. His sense of the holy is bound up with recollection of that event and of the person who embodied it. My sense of the holy, insofar as I have one, is bound up with the hope that someday, any millennium now, my remote descendants will live in a global civilization in which love is pretty much the only law. In such a society, communication would be domination-free, class and caste would be unknown, hierarchy would be a matter of temporary pragmatic convenience, and power would be entirely at the disposal of the free agreement of a literate and well-educated electorate.

I have no idea how such a society could come about. It is, one might say, a mystery. This mystery, like that of the Incarnation, concerns the coming into existence of a love that is kind, patient, and endures all things. 1 Corinthians 13 is an equally useful text for both religious people like Vattimo, whose sense of what transcends our present condition is bound up with a feeling of dependence, and for nonreligious people like myself, for whom this sense consists simply in hope for a better human future. The difference between these two sorts of people is that between unjustifiable gratitude and unjustifiable hope. This is not a matter of conflicting beliefs about what really exists and what does not.

Notes

1. I have argued this point in some detail in an essay on William James's "The Will to Believe": "Religious Faith, Intellectual Responsibility, and Romance," included in my *Philosophy and Social Hope* (New York: Penguin, 1999). Also see my "Pragmatism as Romantic Polytheism," in *The Revival of Pragmatism*, ed. Morris Dickstein (Durham, N.C.: Duke University Press, 1998), 21–36.

2. Of course, we anticlericalists who are also leftists in politics have a further reason for hoping that institutionalized religion will eventually

disappear. We think otherworldliness dangerous because, as John Dewey put it, "Men have never fully used the powers they possess to advance the good in life, because they have waited upon some power external to themselves and to nature to do the work they are responsible for doing" ("A Common Faith," in *Later Works of John Dewey*, vol. 9 [Carbondale and Edwardsville: Southern Illinois University Press, 1986], 31.)

3. This book has appeared in English as *Belief*, trans. Luca D'Isanto and David Webb (Stanford, Calif.: Stanford University Press, 1999). Quotations from Vattimo followed by page numbers in parentheses refer to that volume.

4. Vattimo, "The Trace of the Trace," in *Religion: Cultural Memory in the Present*, ed. Jacques Derrida and Gianni Vattimo, trans. David Webb (Stanford, Calif.: Stanford University Press, 1998), 84.

5. The question of whether this retreat is desirable is quite different from the Kant-style question "is religious belief cognitive or noncognitive?" My distinction between the epistemic arena and what lies outside it is not drawn on the basis of a distinction between human faculties nor of a theory about the way in which the human mind is related to reality. It is a distinction between topics on which we are entitled to ask for universal agreement and other topics. Which topics these are—what should be in the epistemic arena and what should not—is a matter of cultural politics. Prior to what Jonathan Israel calls "the radical Enlightenment," it was assumed that religion was a topic of the former sort. Thanks to three hundred and fifty years of culture-political activity, this is no longer the case. For more on the relation between theology and cultural politics, see my essay "Cultural Politics and the Question of the Existence of God," in *Radical Interpretation in Religion*, ed. Nancy Frankenberry (New York: Cambridge University Press, 2002), 53–77.

It is also a different question than the one about whether religious voices should be heard in the public square where citizens deliberate on political questions. The latter question has been intensively discussed by Stephen Carter, Robert Audi, Nicholas Wolterstorff, and many others. I comment on this debate in my "Religion in the Public Square: A Reconsideration," *Journal of Religious Ethics* 31, no. 1 (Spring 2003): 141–49.

The Age of Interpretation

Gianni Vattimo

THE PHILOSOPHICAL TRUTH of hermeneutics, namely its claim to be a more "valid" thought than other philosophies—for example, to be a more "truthful" philosophy than neo-empiricism or historical materialism, et cetera—evidently cannot be maintained on the basis of a description of what, according to it, the state of affairs really is. That, as Nietzsche writes, "there are no facts, only interpretations," is not an objective, metaphysical proposition. This proposition too is "only" an interpretation. If one reflects on the meaning of this statement, one realizes how much hermeneutics has (in deed) changed the reality of things and transformed philoso-

phy. As is well known, Martin Heidegger, right from the beginning of his career and then more and more consistently and
deliberately in the subsequent elaboration of his thought, did
not provide "proofs" for his propositions. Instead, he put
them forth as responses to situations in which it—his thinking,
he himself—found itself involved, thrown into. The existential
analytic of *Being and Time* does not constitute a description of
the nature and structure of human existence; it is already, in
every sense, an interpretation, that is to say, a listening and a
replying to what we ourselves are, while we are, and entirely
from within. If there is a difference between an "early" and a
"late" Heidegger (a difference for that matter recognizable in
Heidegger's own terminological usage), it lies in an increasingly explicit awareness that the Being, into which we are
thrown and to which we respond from within, is intensely
characterized in historical terms. Thus in the late Heidegger
one seldom or never finds the term "*Eigentlichkeit*" [authentic-
ity]"; however, the etymological root "*eigen*" is still used to characterize the *Ereignis*, the appropriating event of Being. This
observation, which might seem reducible to the level of a
mere lexical accident, expresses rather well the general meaning of the ontological radicalization undergone by hermeneutics in the development of Heidegger's thought.

What I wish to bring out by analyzing the situation in which
we find ourselves placed, on the basis of the results of the existential analytic, is the following: (a) The existential analytic
(section 1 of *Being and Time*) makes us aware that knowledge is
always interpretation and nothing but this. Things appear to us
in the world only because we are in their midst and always
already oriented toward seeking a specific meaning for them.
In other words, we possess a preunderstanding that makes us
interested subjects rather than neutral screens for an objective
overview. And (b) interpretation is the only *fact* of which we can
speak. As one of the classic authors of twentieth-century

hermeneutics, Luigi Pareyson, wrote: "the 'object' manifests itself to the degree to which the 'subject' expresses his or herself, and vice versa." I am not espousing some kind of empirical idealism à la Berkeley. In interpretation the world is given, there are not "subjective" images alone. Yet the Being of things (the ontic reality) is inseparable from the being-there of the human being. Both points, (a) and (b), may also be maintained without too much difficulty from a Kantian perspective. Nevertheless, the claim that the knowing subject is not a neutral screen but an interested subject is already a departure from Kant's teaching; above all, it opens the way for point (c), which I would like to stress, namely that the more we try to grasp interpretation in its authenticity (*Eigentlichkeit*), the more it manifests itself in its eventlike, historical character (*ereignishaft*). Then, (d): if the statement that "there are no facts, but only interpretations" is, as Nietzsche lucidly recognized, an interpretation too, then this interpretation can only be argued as an interested response to a particular historical situation—not as the objective registration of a fact that remains external to it but as itself a fact that enters into the makeup of the very historical situation to which it co-responds.

What I mean, expressed more concisely, is that one cannot talk with impunity of interpretation; interpretation is like a virus or even a *pharmakon* that affects everything it comes into contact with. On the one hand, it reduces all reality to message—erasing the distinction between *Natur* and *Geisteswissenschaften*, since even the so-called hard sciences verify and falsify their statements only within paradigms or preunderstandings. If "facts" thus appear to be nothing but interpretations, interpretation, on the other hand, presents itself as (the) fact: hermeneutics is not a philosophy but the enunciation of historical existence itself in the age of the end of metaphysics. The "validity" of Heidegger's thought is equivalent to its capacity, superior to that of other philosophies, to correspond to the epoch, to let the event speak: the same event that Nietzsche calls nihilism and that for Heidegger is the end of metaphysics. This event comprises the end of Eurocentrism, the critique of ideology, the dissolution of the evidentness of consciousness through psychoanalysis, the explicit pluralization of the agencies of information, the mass media, which, as Heidegger had anticipated in his essay, "The Age of the World-Picture" ("Die Zeit des Weltbildes"), make the idea of a "unique" world picture impossible. Lyotard later labeled all this the end of the metanarratives. Nevertheless, the part of Heidegger's doctrine that we must not forget, but that Lyotard overlooked, is that the end of the metanarratives is not the unveiling of a "true" state of affairs in which the metanarratives "no longer are"; it is, on the contrary, a process of which, given that we are fully immersed in it and cannot regard it from outside, we are called upon to grasp a guiding thread that we can use in order to project its further development; that is, to remain inside it as interpreters rather than as objective recorders of facts.

Lyotard and other theoreticians of postmodernism have neither noticed nor stated, however, that Nietzsche and Heidegger speak not only from within the modern process of dissolution of the metanarratives but above all from within the biblical tradition. It is not so very absurd to assert that the death of God announced by Nietzsche is, in many ways, the death of Christ on the cross told by the Gospels. Elsewhere, I have stressed the significance of Dilthey's reconstruction of the history of metaphysics in his *Introduction to the Human Sciences* (*Einleitung in die Geisteswissenschaften*, 1883).[1] According to Dilthey, it is the advent of Christianity that makes possible the progressive dissolution of metaphysics that, from his perspective, culminates in Kant but that is also Nietzsche's nihilism and Heidegger's end of metaphysics. Christianity introduces into the world the principle of interiority, on the basis of which "objective" reality gradually loses its preponderant weight. What Nietzsche's statement that "there are no facts, only interpretations" and Heidegger's hermeneutic ontology actually do is to draw the extreme consequences from this principle. So the relationship between modern hermeneutics and the history of Christianity is not limited to the fact that reflection on interpretation has an essential nexus with the reading of biblical texts, as has often been observed. Rather, what I am suggesting here is that hermeneutics—expressed in its most radical form in Nietzsche's statement and in Heidegger's ontology—is the development and maturation of the Christian message.

The title "The Age of Interpretation" summarizes the general, ontological aspects of what I've said so far (and which I have discussed more extensively in *After Christianity*). What I would like to develop now, from these premises, is the relationship between the two aspects of the link between hermeneutics and Christianity that I have just mentioned and that seem to me specifically relevant to this essay. What is the relationship between hermeneutics as a technique and discipline of interpretation (from Luther's *sola scriptura* to Schleiermacher and Dilthey) and hermeneutics as a radically "nihilist" ontology, in the sense conveyed by Nietzsche's and Heidegger's assertions? More concretely: What does hermeneutic ontology tell us about the reading and interpretation of biblical texts, about their presence and meaning in the existence of our societies? Can we really argue, as I believe we must, that postmodern nihilism constitutes the actual truth of Christianity?

If we look at the history of the modern churches—and here I am speaking mainly of the Catholic Church, though I may not be far off as regards the history of other Christian confessions as well—it is plain enough that the main challenge faced by the Church has been science's claim to be regarded as the

47

only source of truth. The debates on miracles, on the very possibility of demonstrating the existence of God, and on the reconciliation of divine omnipotence and omniscience with human freedom have always been inspired by the idea that the truth that shall make us free—as Scripture says—could only be the objective truth. The Church too adopted this conception of truth more or less explicitly, with the consequence that it had to attribute objective truth to the statements of the Bible, even ones that expressed the astronomy and cosmology of the ancient world (in the case of Galileo and heliocentrism, for example, Joshua's command to the sun, outside Jericho's wall, to cease moving). Naturally, the Church's "literalism" changed over time, owing in part to a hermeneutic that grew increasingly attentive to the "spiritual" meanings of Scripture. But at the same time, both to respond to the challenge presented by modern science and to lay the foundations for preaching Christianity to far-flung areas and cultures, the Church elaborated a whole doctrine of *preambula fidei*, entangling itself more and more in a metaphysics of the objectivist kind, which by now—as we see even in recent encyclopedias—has become inseparable from the authoritarian claim to preach laws and principles that are natural, hence valid for all and not for the faithful alone. The disputes that are arising in many countries all over the world concerning bioethics constitute the terrain on which the Church's claim to speak in the name of humanity, rather than in the name of a positive revelation, is made most forcefully. The consequence of this may well be the occurrence of further "Galileo cases" and other confrontations between ecclesiastical authority and the contemporary world, owing purely to the stubborn faith of the Church in the contents of a culture that is certainly more ancient and habitual but that has no claim to be considered the eternal truth. Here it suffices to cite the notorious example of the denial of the priesthood to women, which the pope defends not so much on the basis of opportunistic reasons or historical custom, as would be understandable, but by reference to women's "natural" vocation, a notion that at this point can only be taken seriously from a metaphysical and essentialist position. Problems involving its relationship to science, or to demands for emancipation, as in the case of feminism, are not the only ones the Church faces today. There is also, and perhaps mainly, the ecumenical problem—not only among Christian confessions but also among the religions generally. As long as the Church remains trapped in the web of its "natural metaphysics" and its literalism (God is "father," and not mother, for example?), it will never be able to dialogue freely and fraternally, not just with the other Christian confessions but above all with other major world religions. The only way open to the Church not to revert to being the tiny fundamentalist sect it necessarily was at the beginning of its history, but to develop its universal vocation, is to assume the evangelical message as the principle that dissolves all claims to objectivity. It is not a scandal to say that we do not believe in the gospel because we know that Christ is risen, but rather, that we believe that Christ is risen because we have read it in the gospel. This reversal is indispensable if we are to avoid falling into a ruinous realism, into objectivism, and into its corollary, the authoritarianism that has characterized the history of the Church. A statement such as this becomes possible precisely in the age of interpretation, when—according to my hypothesis—Christianity has brought to bear its full antimetaphysical effect, and "reality" in all its aspects has been reduced to message. In this process of reduction there are two inseparable elements: Christianity only makes sense if reality is not first and foremost the world of things at hand (*vorhanden*), objectively present; and the meaning of Christianity as a message of salvation consists above all in dissolving the peremptory claims of "reality." Paul's sentence, "Oh death where is thy victory?"

G I A N N I   V A T T I M O

can rightfully be read as an extreme denial of the "reality principle."

It is difficult to grasp and express all the possible implications of these premises. For example, one of these implications could be summed up with Wittgenstein's phrase that
philosophy (for us, this would be the postmetaphysical philosophy made possible by Christ) can only free us from idols. A
task not irrelevant at all in our contemporary world, even at
the level of politics: the idols include the laws of the market-
place and the purportedly natural rules that prevent the passage of more humane and fraternal legislation (for example,
in Italy and elsewhere we have the problem of same-sex
unions) or even the drive for domination on the part of this or
that group of "technocrats," of experts, of people who feel
entitled to decide on our behalf. In general, a democratic
regime needs a non-objective-metaphysical conception of
truth; otherwise, it immediately becomes an authoritarian
regime. Should it recognize that the redemptive meaning of
the Christian message makes its impact precisely by dissolving
the claims of objectivity, the church might also finally heal the
tension between truth and charity that has, so to speak, tor-
mented it throughout its history. The traditional Aristotelian
slogan "*amicus Plato sed magis amica veritas*" can no longer hold
good for Christians. A character in Dostoevsky says, if I had to
choose between Christ and truth, I would choose Christ. But
the alternative vanishes if we grant all the consequences of the
biblical message. The truth that, according to Jesus, shall
make us free is not the objective truth of science or even that
of theology: likewise, the Bible is not a cosmological treatise or
a handbook of anthropology or theology. The scriptural revelation was not delivered to give us knowledge of how we are,
what God is like, what the "natures" of things or the laws of
geometry are, and so on, as if we could be saved through the
"knowledge" of truth. The only truth revealed to us by Scrip-

ture, the one that can never be demythologized in the course of time—since it is not an experimental, logical, or metaphysical statement but a call to practice—is the truth of love, of charity.

In contemporary postmetaphysical philosophy, including the neopragmatism of Rorty or the philosophy of communicative action of Habermas, the proximity of truth to charity is anything but an extravagant idea. For both thinkers, and for many of our contemporaries, no experience of truth can exist without some kind of participation in a community, and not necessarily the closed community (parish, province, or family) of the communitarians. As in the case of Gadamer's hermeneutics, truth comes about as the ongoing construction of communities that coincide in a "fusion of horizons" (*Horizontverschmelzung*), which has no insuperable "objective" limit (like that of race, language, or "natural" belongings). What appears to be increasingly obvious in contemporary postmetaphysical thought is that truth does not consist in the correspondence between propositions and things. Even when we speak of correspondence, we have in mind propositions verified in the context of paradigms, the truth of which consists above all in their being shared by a community.

I said above that from the perspective that I propose here, postmodern nihilism (the end of metanarratives) is the truth of Christianity. Which is to say that Christianity's truth appears to be the dissolution of the (metaphysical) truth concept itself. But then, to come quickly to the conclusion, why are we still speaking of Christianity? My friend Richard Rorty has expressed his sympathy for my reading of *kenosis* (the incarnation as God's renunciation of his own sovereign transcendence), though without finding in it any reason to feel any closer to Christianity. Now, without in the least wishing to convert Rorty, I do maintain that—as in the case of Nietzsche and Heidegger—even his nonfoundationalism is possible—presentable as a reasonable thesis—only because we are living in a civilization shaped by the biblical, and specifically Christian message. If this were not the case, Rorty would, paradoxically, be obliged to supply demonstrative proof for his nonfoundationalism as an "objective" thesis, that is, to argue that *in reality* there are no foundations—forgetting the additional clause in Nietzsche's sentence: "there are no facts, only interpretations; *and this is an interpretation.*" Naturally, in putting this point to Rorty, I am taking what he does not explicitly articulate to the extreme. From a pragmatic perspective, he is consistent in not offering objective-metaphysical proofs, but he does acknowledge a spontaneous preference for a worldview that rejects foundationalism and is thus more desirable inasmuch as less authoritarian and more open to human freedom. But what can we do when we find this spontaneous preference for a more humane and democratic society lacking? Do we merely acknowledge the insurmountable condition of belonging to different communities? There is a third possibility between, on one hand, the metaphysical demonstration of the truth of Christianity (the *preambula fidei* and the historical veracity of the resurrection) and, on the other, its falseness with respect to scientific reason (entailing the quasi-naturalistic acceptance of the differences among individuals, cultures, and societies): Christianity as a historical message of salvation. Those who followed Christ when he appeared to them in Palestine did not do so because they had seen him perform miracles, and even less had all those who followed him subsequently done so. They believed, as we say in Italian, "*sulla parola,*" that is, "they took him at his word"; they had "*fides ex auditu,*" faith from hearing. The commitment to Christ's teaching derives from the cogency of the message itself; he who believes has understood, felt, intuited that his word is a "word of eternal life."

At a time when, thanks to the Christianity that has permeated the history of our institutions as well as the history of our culture more generally, we have come to realize that the experience of truth is above all that of hearing and interpreting messages (even in the "hard sciences" there are paradigms, preunderstandings that we receive as messages), the Christian revelation has cogency insofar as we recognize that without it our historical existence would not make sense. The example of the "classics" of a literature, a language, a culture is illuminating here. Just as western literature would not be thinkable without its Homeric poems, without Shakespeare and Dante, our culture in its broadest sense would not make sense if we were to remove Christianity from it.

The authority of an such an argument seems insufficient only because we have not yet fully developed the antimetaphysical consequences of Christianity itself; because we are not yet nihilistic enough, in other words Christian enough, we still oppose the historical-cultural cogency of the biblical tradition to a "natural reality" that supposedly exists independently of it and with respect to which the biblical truth is obliged to "prove itself." But must we really believe in Jesus Christ only if we are able to demonstrate that God created the world in seven days or that Jesus himself actually rose on Easter morning and by extension that man is by nature one thing or another or that the family is by nature monogamous and heterosexual, that matrimony is by nature indissoluble, that woman is incapable by nature of entering the priestly office, and so on? It is far more reasonable to believe that our existence depends on God because here, today, we are unable to speak our language and to live out our historicity without responding to the message transmitted to us by the Bible. One might object that this is still a specific belonging, which forgets humanity in general and closes itself off from other religions and cultures. Yet these consequences follow even more certainly if we take the Christian revelation to be tied to a natural metaphysics, which, in the wake of the marxist critique of ideology and cultural anthropology, appears as anything but "natural."

So, with respect to Rorty's pragmatism, what I propose is an explicit appropriation of our Christian historicity. This is what Benedetto Croce meant when he wrote that "we cannot not call ourselves Christians." Perhaps this expression should be taken in its literal sense, even underscoring the words "call ourselves": as soon as we try to account for our existential condition, which is never generic or metaphysical but always historical and concrete, we discover that we cannot place ourselves outside the tradition opened up by the proclamation of Christ. True, one cannot guarantee that nonbelievers would be persuaded by such an argument. It is something more, however, than an acknowledgment of an insurmountable limit that can only be regulated by reciprocal tolerance—because for that matter there is very often no reciprocity at all. Today, when all claims by historical authorities to command in the name of truth have been revealed as deceptions that absolutely cannot be tolerated in a democracy, Croce's assertion should perhaps be interpreted in the same sense, between despair and invocation, as Heidegger's statement that "only a god can save us [*Nur noch ein Gott kann un retten*]." "We cannot not call ourselves Christians" because in a world where God is dead—where the metanarratives have been dissolved and all authority has fortunately been demythologized, including that of "objective" knowledge—our only chance of human survival rests in the Christian commandment of charity.

Note

1. G. Vattimo, *After Christianity*, trans. Luca D'Isanto (New York: Columbia University Press, 2002).

What is Religion's Future
After Metaphysics?

Richard Rorty, Gianni Vattimo, and Santiago Zabala

Paris, 16 December 2002

SANTIAGO ZABALA: Before discussing the future of religion,
I would like to talk about "weak thought" and its postmetaphysical culture. What you both have been working
on was the paradigm shift from metaphysics to "weak
thought," which today is best represented by pragmatism
and hermeneutics. The metaphysical tradition was dominated by the thought that there is something nonhuman
that human beings should try to live up to—a thought
that today finds its most plausible expression in the scien-

tistic conception of culture. James and Dewey stand with Nietzsche and Heidegger in asking us to abandon this tradition and culture. Even if Cartesian and Hegelian thought has completed its parabola and the linguistic turn in philosophy has led us away from epistemology and metaphysics, it seems impossible to cut oneself off completely from the metaphysical Logos. Is this the reason why the moral concern of pragmatism and hermeneutics today is to continue and promote the impulse to conversation of the West rather than to ask metaphysical questions about what is or is not real? Is this what "weak thought" is all about?

RICHARD RORTY: Cutting oneself off from the metaphysical Logos is pretty much the same thing as ceasing to look for power and instead being content with charity. The gradual movement within Christianity in recent centuries in the direction of the social ideals of the Enlightenment is a sign of the gradual weakening of the worship of God as power and its gradual replacement with the worship of God as love. I think of the decline of the metaphysical Logos as a decline in the intensity of our attempt to participate in power and in grandeur. The transition from power to charity and that from the metaphysical Logos to postmetaphysical thought are both expressions of a willingness to take one's chances, as opposed to attempting to escape one's finitude by aligning oneself with infinite power.

SANTIAGO ZABALA: So "the end of metaphysics" and Gadamer's famous slogan, "Being that can be understood is language," are not final discoveries about the intrinsic nature of Being but rather suggestions about how to redescribe the process of our understanding? It seems that, to put the point in Robert Brandom's Hegelian way, to understand the nature of an object is only to be able to recapitulate the history of the concept of that object?

GIANNI VATTIMO: I don't know how far the idealistic element in pragmatism goes because even when you speak of "describing the way things are," it is not a description at all; it is already something that has more to do with practice and interhuman relationships than with the description even of some process. So the problem is how far can we imagine that this new postmetaphysical attitude leaves aside completely the ideal real world "out there"? ("Out there" is an expression I've learned from Richard.) In this way, the transformation is more radical than what we expected because at the very beginning, when pragmatism was taught in Europe it just appeared to be a sort of American practical way of treating things: it does not matter what things are in themselves, it is more important what they mean for us or what we do with them and so on. It seems to me that the implications of all these theses, of this pragmatic attitude, are more or less the same as the development of Heidegger's philosophy. In *Sein und Zeit* Heidegger appeared to be a sort of pragmatist existential philosopher: things have no essence of themselves, but they appear, they come to "Being" in the way in which they come to a project, a shared project (and so also for language). But after he started to take more seriously the notion of "ontological difference," since "Being" is not what is already there but, on the contrary, it is what happens in everyday dialogue among humans. So there also seems to be an "ontological implication" in the pragmatist starting point of Heidegger. In these ontological implications of pragmatism, Heidegger could also appear as somebody who took radically what pragmatism means for "Being" itself; even if pragmatically we could also no longer speak of "Being" in itself. There is a sort of self-contradictory ontology in Heidegger. Ontology means that we want to speak about Being, but Being is nothing but the Logos interpreted as dialogue, *Gespräch*, as the actual discussion among people. So reality still has a meaning in Heidegger, but it is just the result of the historical dialogue among people; we don't agree because we have found the very essence of reality, but we say that we have found the very essence of reality when we agree.

RICHARD RORTY: I agree. That seems just the right way to put it. What was true in idealism was that inquiry is a matter of finding coherence among beliefs, not of corresponding to an object. Robert Brandom's neo-Hegelianism (which can be described either as a version of pragmatism or as a version of idealism) entails that there is no such thing as getting the world right or getting Being right. We can, to be sure, get particular things right—planetary motions or constitutional government, for example—since what counts as getting them right is specified by the language games we know how to play. But each philosopher makes up his own game, his own private little language game, when he talks of something as unspecific and as unrelated to practice as "the world" or "Being." Brandom's synthesis of pragmatism and idealism gives us a philosophical position that combines Hegel without eschatology and Heidegger without ontology.

GIANNI VATTIMO: The question becomes, What criteria do we have for launching a dialogue? There are some differences between arbitrariness and agreement. Agreement is always related to a sort of continuity: we agree on what we find true and to find something true is to apply criteria of some kind, paradigms that are not completely arbitrarily chosen but that are somehow found. This is, for instance, the difference I see between Gadamer's hermeneutics and Wittgenstein's language games, because in Wittgenstein's language games you have the "game" and the "rules" of the game that you must play following the rules to agree with other people, but it is hermeneutics that tries to make evident and clarify the historicity of the rules. So, even if there is no objective Logos of the nature of reality, every time we agree on something we actually give a sort of testimony, we realize a sort of continuity of the Logos, which is the only criterion we actually have. This is the reason why I insist on charity, because charity could be thought of as a metarule that obliges and pushes us to accept the different language games, the different rules of the language games.

RICHARD RORTY: The term "language game" may have been unfortunate because it suggested a rule-governed procedure. I think Wittgenstein at his best rejected the notion of rules in favor of the notions of practices, traditions, the kind of things that people pick up by participating without learning any rules but just by "know-how." One might think of charity as the willingness to pick up other people's practices, to gain other people's "know-how." Arbitrariness, from this point of view, is the conviction that one's own social practice is the only social practice one will ever need and that one does not need to fuse horizons with anybody else because one's own social practice is already sufficient.

GIANNI VATTIMO: In studying and trying to think hermeneutically, I have always had the impression that hermeneutics also involves a sort of weakening of subjectivity; for instance, when we think about practices, shared criteria, traditions, and so on, we tend to react with a defense of the originality and the autonomy of subjectivity, as in the revolutionary attitude, the revolutions in science, for example. How can we hold together these two aspects of the fact that my subjectivity is not so essential because in all I do language speaks through me and in me and, on the other side, I am a subject? But if I were not a subject there would be no history of language because language is made by *langue et parole*. So, how should we see this question that is always asked, again and again, also against hermeneutics? Richard, you are a traditionalist, you risk a conformism if everything that is said is to be agreed with other people.

RICHARD RORTY: I've been writing about that sort of question lately. I try to distinguish between the kind of grandeur that is associated with onto-theology—the grandeur of something all-encompassing, something that provides the largest possible framework of discourse and sets the bounds for all thoughts—and what Isaiah Berlin calls "romantic profundity." I agree with Berlin when he says that the romantics were the first people to question the metaphysical notion of grandeur. They suggested dropping the notion of something high and vast and remote and replacing it with the notion of something deep within—the source of poetic inspiration. But from the point of view of postmetaphysical thought, infinite depth is as bad an idea as infinite power. Instead of getting in touch with either, postmetaphysical thinkers just want to make finite little changes. They are piecemeal reformers rather than intellectual revolutionaries. Instead of saying that their ideas reflect something grand or stem from something profound, they put forward their ideas as suggestions that might be of use for certain particular purposes.

GIANNI VATTIMO: Yes, I agree, and this could also be the meaning of the insistence of Gadamer on the classics, because the classics are something that has become a model without having any foundations; even if we assume that Homer's poems have become classics for some reason, it just means that they are classics, it does not mean that they come from any foundation.

RICHARD RORTY: Right, they are classics because of the effect they have on us, not because of the source they came from.

GIANNI VATTIMO: This is also the meaning of the *Ereignis* in many ways, the idea that Being is the event, just what happened. But nevertheless, the problem of subjectivity in a way is always the interpretation of continuity; for instance, when I have a conversation with you and Santiago, I have to decide whether I accept one's opinion or the other's. In this there isn't simply innovation, something new in the conversation, because even Hitler could be considered "new" in the conversation. This is what I always raise against Derrida when he says "provided that 'the other' is something really important." But the otherness of Nazism was very profound. Derrida always wants to show that it wasn't so new because if it was very new, it could be considered as the messiah. So, there is always again and again this problem of deciding on which basis I must accept or refuse one of your points. We always put into action a system of criteria that validate themselves only *après coup*, only if they work in the conversation and only if what I say can become a small classic between us. This would be another implication of the notion of Being as an event . . .

SANTIAGO ZABALA: According to your hypothesis, Professor Vattimo, Christianity will only attain all its antimetaphysical consequences in our Age of Interpretation by reducing "reality" to "message," and if we haven't yet developed fully the antimetaphysical consequences of Christianity, it is because we are not yet "nihilistic enough." Can you please explain what you mean by "nihilistic enough?"

GIANNI VATTIMO: The answer to this question depends again very much on the history of metaphysics, which I've learned from Heidegger and Dilthey. Basically, I share the idea that ancient metaphysics was deeply objective and platonic, where the ideas were to be contemplated as essences; this, of course, is already an interpretation we give of ancient metaphysics because nobody would assume that either the description of Hegel or the description of Dilthey, which depends on it, is an objective description of what ancient metaphysics actually was. For instance, I have the tendency now to bring back all these stories to the relations of power, which is not, I think, a case of ingenuous naive marxism, but it is a matter of considering the ancient society in which just a small group of people had power and the others were slaves. Metaphysics has survived because (and together with) the ancient structure of "power" has survived. So, for instance, the Christian church, being the head of the Roman Empire, could not abandon this structure of power and was not able to develop all the antimetaphysical implications of Christianity. I see a possible reduction of metaphysics to the structure of power, even if Heidegger would not agree completely because he would say that it was thanks to metaphysics that the structure of power remains the same. I do not assume that there is a simple cause and an effect, but there is a togetherness of the history of Being. On the other side, this reduction can not be expanded to the point of saying that if the ancient structure of power had not been the way it is, we would have had a new metaphysical epoch earlier, a more realistic and authentic one; this in not case. Again, the problem we are always confronted with is the idea of taking radically enough the idea of the "eventuality of Being," the "event" character of Being, because on the contrary we would be able to say that if power had not been the way it was, then we would already have a sort of authentic humanity. But this was not the case because what actually happened to us has more to do with historicity than anything else. Is there any cutoff point in history? This is my question and problem as a Christian because when I say that "thanks to God I am an atheist" and I have become an atheist thanks to Jesus' existence, "thanks to Jesus" implies that I accept that there is a sort of cutoff point in history: B.C. before and A.D. after. If I do not accept this radical historicity, I find myself again in the situation of having to admit a sort of basic, authentic, realistic, stable structure of reality that I discover at a certain point. That there is no metaphysical foundation is still a foundation. If I accept radically my historicity, I do not see any other possibility than to speak of religion. This is why I speak of religion, of accepting this structure without meeting a sort religious history of foundation, because if I were not a Christian I would probably be a metaphysician. When Nietzsche says "God is dead," it does not mean that God does not exist because this would imply again a sort of metaphysical thesis on the structure of reality. The difficulty I find in being radically historicist and not having any foundation is that it can only be accepted reasonably if I attribute this history to a sort of transcendental dialogue that is between me and the history of foundations and God, otherwise everything would be a guide throughout history. So, when I say that "thanks to God I am an atheist," "thanks to God" is very important, it means thanks to the history of the revelation, the salvation, the dissolution of Being that I'm an atheist and this history actually is my paradoxical foundation.

SANTIAGO ZABALA: Nietzsche said, "I fear that we shall be unable to get rid of God, since we still believe in grammar." Are we supposed to interpret this negatively or positively?

GIANNI VATTIMO: This could be taken not only negatively but also positively as long as we are a *Gespräch*.

SANTIAGO ZABALA: So, from a pragmatic and hermeneutical point of view this sentence has a positive and not a negative meaning because of the end of metaphysics?

GIANNI VATTIMO: Absolutely, this sentence applies to hermeneutics and pragmatism because these are two philosophical points of view that could not exist without a sort of religious implication. I'm not sure if Richard agrees with me on this point?

RICHARD RORTY: Let me first say something about the relation between ancient Greek society and the metaphysical tradition. Dewey insisted that the former be related to the latter, and I think he had a good point. In *The Quest for Certainty* and *Reconstruction in Philosophy*, Dewey asks us to think of philosophical contemplation, *theoria*, as an ideal appropriate for a leisure class that was hoping to take over leadership from the warrior class. It was an ideal appropriate for a time when Athens was powerful and at peace and when all the hard work was done by slaves. But the need for such an ideal need not produce onto-theology, as is shown, perhaps, by looking at ancient China. There you had a leisure class that did not produce onto-theology. Contemporary sinologists say: Isn't Confucianism wonderful because it isn't metaphysical! If they are right about this, then it suggests that what is common to Greek onto-theology and the Confucian tradition is that both purport to put you in touch with something that is neither historically determined nor conversationally alterable. The Chinese apparently managed to engage in that project without what we call metaphysics, but they still managed it.

On the question of a decisive event in history, the big difference between Gianni and me is that I am not really impressed by the B.C.-A.D. distinction. For me, the decisive events occurred in the late eighteenth century A.D., when the French Revolution coincided with the romantic movement. The intellectuals began talking about the power of the human imagination, as Schiller and Shelley did, at the same time that Christian charity changed into *liberté, egalité, fraternité*. That constellation of events is the one that captures my imagination.

SANTIAGO ZABALA: But isn't there a connection between democracy and Christianity, between religion and politics? Being a religious person should not be very different from being a democratic citizen. Even if Jefferson thought that it was enough to privatize religion, to view it as irrelevant to social order, he did, though, think it was essential for individual perfection.

RICHARD RORTY: Jefferson is not very clear about the extent to which he thought religion optional, but I doubt that he would have said it was essential for individual perfection.

SANTIAGO ZABALA: But today, after metaphysics, there is a difference for the religious person in the way this perfection works, whether he or she believes in an ontological God or a weak God. Heidegger himself at the end of *Contributions to Philosophy (From Enowning)* talks about the "Last God." What I would like to know is: How does weak thought work with the end of metaphysics from a religious point of view? There is a connection that you both pointed out in your essays.

GIANNI VATTIMO: In trying to show that I could not be a hermeneutical or pragmatic philosopher without being a Christian there is still a sort of missionary attitude, as though I wished to convert Richard; so when you formulate the question in terms of "religious persons" and "pragmatist persons" who can work together side by side on the basis of different ontological interpretations of something, it is really what I think I still have to develop as a Christian. A nonmetaphysical religiousness is also a nonmissionary one. Nietzsche says somewhere that one's salvation does not depend on my act of faith or on my philosophical discoveries; it does not really matter about oneself, about one's salvation. This is another way to describe how it is possible to make a philosophy of the multiplicity of the possible philosophies without claiming to be right or to sum up all the possibilities. When we think that (1) "Being" is an event of the Logos, (2) the Logos is "dialogue," and (3) dialogue is the sum of inter-subjective discourse; then our ontological worry is to be able to "found" Being, not to try to find something that is already there, but construing something that holds, that resists in time. I was surprised by the thesis on salvation that was made by W. Kramer a few months ago in a con-ference in Spain on the Gadamerian sentence "Being that can be understood is language," because he empha-sized that *Sprache* is *Gespräch*, is dialogue, so that Being is not written somewhere in a sort of Chomskian, more his-torically qualified structure of language, but it is just the result of the human dialogue. This seems to me very close to the Christian evangelical dictum "when two or more of you are gathered in my name I will be with them." So, it is just there that God is present, even Jesus says that when you see a poor person at the corner of the street God is there and not somewhere else. Discussing this, I also had some new and less orthodox ideas on the notion of the Eucharist. I feel that the protestant view of the sacrament of the Holy Communion is justified because there is not the real presence in the transubstantiation, all these medieval theories that were thought to support the fetishist notions of Eucharist sacraments in the church. So Christianity, or as you say Richard, the French Revolution and romanticism, have liberated us from the importance of objective ontology and from the importance also of any kind of foundation that is not related to charity. I see here a series of consequences that I have not yet completely developed, so when I say that we are not yet "nihilistic enough," it means that every time we start again to discuss these implications we realize that there are many more implications than the ones we have already imagined and probably they are also strongly political: they have to do with the way we practice and conceive everyday common life because everything is still much too authoritarian in this common life. We cannot think about asking every newborn child about the constitution, for example, because the constitution is already there, but it is possible that being more perfect and less imprecise about democratic structures will involve an increasing capacity of modifying the rules and the acceptance of the rules. I do not know what the consequences may be, but the mediatization of our world involves more and more possibilities for the individual to participate in the definition of the rules, even if we are not sure that all these consequences will be fully developed; but surely these political possibilities are potentially real now. Do I exaggerate the importance of politics in this thought? There is always something else like interiority, *interiore homines animat veritas.* This is exactly the way of realizing that being is *Gespräch,* is dialogue, because the dialogue takes place in political common life. I would not accept the objection made by some colleagues of mine who say that I exaggerate the politicization of philosophy, because the idea that there is a way of experiencing truth beyond social intercourse is already a little bit dubious as a metaphysical separation of essences from the everyday life. This is another way of recognizing that we are not yet "nihilistic enough."

RICHARD RORTY: Robert Brandom has a commentary on Hegel's *Phenomenology* coming out soon, and one of the fundamental thoughts in that book is that the best translation of *Geist*, in the sense in which Hegel uses that word, is conversation.[1] A lot of the resistance among analytic philosophers to Brandom's and my pragmatism is that "conversation" still appears to them as something second-rate, something "weak," in comparison to scientific inquiry. They treat science as an area of culture that reaches out to a goal beyond the merely human. So I find it useful to think of the opposite of analytical philosophy as conversational philosophy. From this point of view, analytic philosophy looks like the last gasp of the onto-theological tradition.

SANTIAGO ZABALA: The pope has recently said, in his visit to the Italian parliament, that the worst enemy of religion is "ethical relativism." It is interesting to notice that we are here moving in the opposite direction.

GIANNI VATTIMO: My basic opinion now is that people hate Christianity because of the priests. I never have an explanation for the fact that preaching a religion of love, charity, pathos, and *misericordia* is not accepted by some people. This is the mystery of the starting chapter of the Gospel according to John; "the partners did not accept." But why is it so difficult to preach Christianity? I think it is because of the Church, but not simply because of the richness of the pope or the corruption of the pedophile priests in the American churches, but because it is too strong a structure. The romantics understood this, for example, in the famous fragments known as the *Älteste Systemprogramm des deutschen Idealismus* of Hegel, Hölderlin, and Schelling, when they spoke of a new religion and a sort of mythological esthetical society; this idea was mostly created against the church, the authoritarian churches. So when we talk about the future of religion I also think about another question: What about the future of the Church, the visible, disciplinary, and dogmatic structure of the Church? Some people have reproached me for still talking about Christianity and not about anything else, but Christianity is something that came to me through Church, tradition, texts . . . so I should always imply that there is something objective in this system because of the way we speak of all the other things, not only of religion. This is the main question: What should I expect as a believer, as a believer to believe, from that aspect of social individual life that is religion? Here I always come back to the example of Comte, who founded a sort of positivistic church because he wanted people to go somewhere on Sundays, at least to do something that had an attitude comparable to religious preaching.

SANTIAGO ZABALA: Can we have a private religion without church then?

GIANNI VATTIMO: I don't think so, not even if there could be philosophers preaching and discussing. It is a very important point to recognize that the history of metaphysics is not restricted to the denotation of the term itself but was involved with the history of social institutions. So we can't leave completely aside the idea that there is a sort of social problem of religion; for instance, one of my students, when I speak against the pope prohibiting prophylactics always asks me, "But what do you expect, that the pope recommend prophylactics?" I always reply that I would prefer him not to speak about this problem at all, but on the other side, I also ask myself what should the pope speak about? This is also a problem about our social grammar. I would like to emphasize that the problem of the future of religion could also be translated into the smaller, but also very important problem, of the future of the Church. For instance the future of art is also related to the future of museums: What do we expect from museums? Do we expect all the paintings of the past to be destroyed by the new creativity? So, there is a sort of parallel between these two aspects of culture.

RICHARD RORTY: One solution is for everybody to go out and found a new church. There is a good book by Harold Bloom called *The American Religion.* He discusses the Mormons, the Christian Scientists, and the Southern Baptists and concludes that there is a great American tradition: "if you do not like the churches, found your own." The motto of the book is that no true American believes himself younger than God.

GIANNI VATTIMO: It is true. All this has to do, again, with institutions and freedom.

RICHARD RORTY: Of course, shortly after one of these private American churches is founded, it develops its own little Vatican and becomes one more horrible authoritarian institution.

GIANNI VATTIMO: Yes, even if you say that *Geist* is basically conversation. This is another aspect of the same problem because *Geist* in Hegel was also the objective *Geist,* the remnant of the creation of the past, the symbolic forms, even the structure of power; so to bring back *Geist* to conversation would mean more or less to bring state institutions back to democracy, it's the same. We have institutions, but they are institutions that we can modify through social intercourse, but still they have to be established again and again, we cannot do without a grammar . . .

RICHARD RORTY: Yes, I agree.

GIANNI VATTIMO: I think this is probably a special character of modernity because, for instance, take the notion of "originality" in art before the Renaissance; they were not so concerned with "original works." The idea of the artist as a genius starts in the Renaissance. This could be our modern predicament, the situation in which we have discovered that we are concerned with creativity and freedom more than in the past. So, we find again and again this sort of paradigmatic wall: we cannot escape the question whether we accept completely the institutions because we'll end up by killing them since institutions are institutions that we instituted and also on the other side if we refuse them completely. So there is a sort of balance between the two points: the Abraham myth read by Kierkegaard was a sort of conflict between the general rule and the personal vocation.

RICHARD RORTY: But Kierkegaard has a taste for dramatization and infinite differences. There is no suggestion that Abraham and God might have talked things over.

GIANNI VATTIMO: Of course, I agree. I think I have recently found a nondramatic interpretation of Kierkegaard's *Abraham* where Abraham, coming back from the experience of Mount Moliah, had to go back to general rules in order to be able to live even if he accepted them only for the sake of God and not for the sake of universality. But anyway he went on not killing his son, which is a sort of ironical possibility.

SANTIAGO ZABALA: Before the Enlightenment we were told that we only had duties to God, and during the Enlightenment we were told that we also had duties to reason, but both the Age of Faith and the Age of Reason were wrong. Today we seem to be in the Age of Interpretation.

What is our duty today? What are the "positive" and the "negative" senses of the deconstruction of the history of ontology regarding faith and belief?

RICHARD RORTY: I think the answer to the question "Where does our duty lie today?" is "Our only duty is to our fellow citizens." You may conceive your fellow citizens as the other Italians, your fellow Europeans, or your fellow humans. But, whatever the boundaries of one's sense of responsibility, this sense of civic responsibility is possible even if you have never heard either of reason or of religious faith. Civic responsibility existed in Athens before Plato invented the thing we now call "reason."

GIANNI VATTIMO: What can we do with people who apparently do not share civic responsibility either inside our society or outside? The West still represents a lot of the international commerce and technological domination in the world. So what happens when we arrive at a place which refuses us, like some parts of the Islamic world, what do you think we should preach to them?

RICHARD RORTY: Europe is not just domination, not just hegemony, not just international capitalism. There is also the European *mission civilizatrice*. That term has been discredited by the behavior of the colonial powers, but it might be capable of being rehabilitated. It was, after all, Europe that invented democracy and civic responsibility. We can still say to the rest of the world: send your people to our universities, learn about our traditions, and eventually you will see the advantage of a democratic way of life. It may be just an historical accident that Christendom was where democracy was reinvented for the use of mass society, or it may be that this could only have happened within a Christian society. But it is futile to speculate about this. However that may be, it seems to me that the idea of a dialogue with Islam is pointless. There was no dialogue between the *philosophes* and the Vatican in the eighteenth century, and there is not going to be one between the mullahs of the Islamic world and the democratic West. The Vatican in the eighteenth century had its own best interests in mind, and the mullahs have theirs. They no more want to be displaced from their positions of power than the Catholic hierarchy did (or does). With luck, the educated middle class of the Islamic countries will bring about an Islamic Enlightenment, but this enlightenment will not have anything much to do with a "dialogue with Islam."

GIANNI VATTIMO: It is interesting also to notice that the people in the rich western countries who do not share the advantages feel like the excluded people of the third-world countries. There is a sort of implicit coalition between the antiglobal protesters in Europe and the antiglobal protesters in the United States.

RICHARD RORTY: I'm very pessimistic about the political future because I think that democracy only works if you spread the wealth around—if you eliminate the gap between the rich and the poor. This has actually been happening in certain small Northern European countries like Holland and Norway. It happened to a limited extent in the United States during the fifties and sixties. But everything changed in the United States around 1973, with the first oil crisis. Since then we have become a more divided and a more selfish country.

SANTIAGO ZABALA: Right, and Nietzsche also said that "Democracy is Christianity made natural."

RICHARD RORTY: He thought that was an insult, but it should be taken as a compliment.

SANTIAGO ZABALA: So may we say that at the end of metaphysics there is a connection between democracy and Christianity? It seems to me that pragmatism and hermeneutics agree on this point after onto-theology. At least your essays also emphasize this connection.

GIANNI VATTIMO: Right! This seems to me very exact.

RICHARD RORTY: Yes, I think the hermeneutical or Gadamerian attitude is in the intellectual world what democracy is in the political world. The two can be viewed as alternative appropriations of the Christian message that love is the only law.

GIANNI VATTIMO: Coming back to what you said before, Richard, spreading wealth around as a condition for democracy is like expanding knowledge or education as a condition for hermeneutics. I always think that I would give my children to somebody who has read the same books I have; this seems to me a moral education.

RICHARD RORTY: Yes, I would too.

GIANNI VATTIMO: So, hermeneutics as a democratic development involves a sort of expansion of our knowledge, education, and texts, even if "ours" is already something dubious. The increasing political incertitude in Europe can also be understood as a doubt about the efficacy of the capitalistic market structure of our society (this is also J. E. Stiglitz's opinion in his latest book on globalization, *Globalization and Its Discontents*). In Italy we now have a crisis in the car industry, in Fiat, and the only solution we really have is to increase our competitiveness, but if we do this we will probably not increase our exports to India, for example. So, the idea of competition, the idea of the economic movement, does not always solve the problem because in the global society it is more difficult to hide the bad effects of market competition.

RICHARD RORTY: Yes, I agree.

GIANNI VATTIMO: It is difficult in Europe today to sell shoes made by Indian children because we know they are being exploited there, so it seems to me that socialism is a sort of necessary result of technological development. Capitalism worked much better when the world was not so unified by information and commerce, but now it becomes difficult to organize a global power with the capacity to exploit or take advantage of the inequality of capitalism.

SANTIAGO ZABALA: Isn't the WTO trying to do this?

GIANNI VATTIMO: Well, this is what the WTO tries to do, they seem to be very liberal, but when the South American countries want to export merchandise to Europe, they can't because they face very high tariffs. I do not know how far my faith in socialism goes.

RICHARD RORTY: I do not have any faith either in socialism or in capitalism. It seems to me that in the industrialized countries capitalism only became tolerable when the state's intervention created the welfare state and thereby brought the capitalists, to some extent, under democratic control. What we are seeing now is that, in the absence of a world government—in the absence of a global authority that could put global capitalism in the service of democracy—all the worst features of capitalism are reemerging. We shouldn't have had economic globalization until we had a bureaucratic structure to regulate global capitalism, in the way that some countries have been able to regulate it within their own borders. We have unfortunately been overtaken by events. I cannot attach any meaning to socialism anymore. I used to think I was a socialist, but now I do not know what a socialist economy would look like. Nobody wants to nationalize the means of production. Everybody thinks of a market economy as indispensable. So I think that we should just explain that "socialism" now means no more than "capitalism tamed."

GIANNI VATTIMO: The idea of an economy governed by politics and not the opposite is still what socialism means. This is the only reason why I can still accept it.

RICHARD RORTY: That's what the Republicans in the U.S. mean by "socialism." That's why they think it is so awful! They can't stand the thought that big businessmen should be seen as having public responsibilities.

GIANNI VATTIMO: And it also seems to me that in a globalized situation it is more difficult to escape from the necessity of a socialized economy.

RICHARD RORTY: Absolutely, if only because there are not going to be any jobs left in Europe and in America. All the work of the world is going to be done in places like Malaysia and Zimbabwe, so there will be no hope for the working classes of the old democracies.

SANTIAGO ZABALA: If Socrates' turn away from the gods, Christianity's turn from an omnipotent Creator to the man who suffered on the cross, and the Baconian turn from science as contemplation of eternal truth to science as instrument of social progress were not made by appealing to "eternal truths" but by the rise of new ways of speaking, new vocabularies which permit things to sound plausible which previously sounded so uncommon, then will the future of religion depend on the substitution of solidarity, charity, and irony for knowledge?

GIANNI VATTIMO: The problem here is what we should call "knowledge," because "solidarity," "charity," and "irony" build up a sort of objective world, objective *Geist*, and so knowledge would be again and again required in order to get into the meaning of what we should do together. Even if the phenomenology of spirit were only to be applied to historical problems, it would still be a phenomenology of spirit; it would still be a process of knowledge, of becoming acquainted with transmitted values and forms. So things do not really change. School, for example, must still be there to create and preserve continuity between Logos, discourse: This is knowledge. I do not think that if one does not believe that there is something out there, knowledge loses its importance, because even when Heidegger says that "science does not think," this only implies that science calculates, but it does not change very much the actual work of the scientists because they are simply reminded that they also have to "think," to discuss the paradigms, to take into account the social consequences of their discoveries, but everything remains more or less the same.

SANTIAGO ZABALA: Yes, but something does change after ontology.

GIANNI VATTIMO: Ontology is not something that concerns objects because objects are not out there, so ontology concerns our way of relating to "Being" and "beings." It's like a critical attitude; not taking as obvious what appears to be obvious because it depends on historical conditions and on social interrelations.

RICHARD RORTY: If you think of knowledge as just the ability to solve problems, as Kuhn did, then you will think of inquiry as going on forever—for we will always have new problems, and will always find new ways to solve them. Progress in plumbing, carpentry, physics, and chemistry will continue forever, unaffected by the death of ontology.

GIANNI VATTIMO: Religion has always implied a sort of feeling of dependence and for me this is still valid because when I speak of the God of the Bible, I speak of the God which I know only through the Bible, which is not a subject outside, because my dependence on God is my dependence only on the biblical tradition, on the fact that in the past they could not think without biblical conditions and meanings. So this is my creatural feeling, I depend on it, and I can't do without it. Is this also a way of loving God? Yes, because love is a sort of feeling of dependence that is not involved with a pathology; one does not revolt against the feeling of dependence one has in relation to people one loves, and this has serious implications in our social life and so on. . . . Is there any feeling of dependence that one could not consider pathological?

RICHARD RORTY: The only book Dewey wrote about religion was called *A Common Faith*. At the end of that book he says there we can experience a sense of integration into a community of causes that joins the human with the non-human universe. This kind of vague romantic pantheism, Dewey thought, is the only expression of a sense of dependence we need—recognizing that we are part of a larger whole. You can think of this larger whole in many different ways: as the books you read or your cultural tradition or the physical universe. Or you can go back and forth between one such whole and others, depending on how your imagination works.

GIANNI VATTIMO: This attitude has been reused again and again through history by the church only because of metaphysical strategies. When I listen to you, Richard, I do not, as a believer in what I believe, feel that you are very different from me and from what the Church could be, could preach, so this is why the churches probably defend their dogmatisms by saying that you need "a gun to kill a mosquito": if you do not preach big dogmatic values, you do not persuade anybody.

RICHARD RORTY: Yes, it's true.

GIANNI VATTIMO: This is the only way they could justify this vague pantheistic attitude, which I call "half-believer"; but the church believes that it is necessary to emphasize more the fact that there is a God or that you will be punished. . . . This is another way of becoming "nihilistic enough," through the knowledge of our contextual traditions, reading also Buddhist or Indian books. I do not feel that what you say, Richard, is so un-Christian, but the problem is that it is un-Christian for Christians because of the metaphysical strength which is often justified as a form of *biblia pauperum*, preaching for poor people. But we cannot consider that the poor are always with us; many times they have become rich because the Church works against itself. When it really works, the Church works against the survival of the Church.

RICHARD RORTY: In your essay "Ethics Without Transcendence?" you make an interesting point about the churches giving up sexual prohibition;[2] I think that if the churches gave up the attempt to dictate sexual behavior they would lose a lot of their reason for existing. What keeps them around is this deep, Freudianly explainable desire for purity, ritual purity. There is something deep to appeal to there, and the churches are good at doing so. But once Christianity is reduced to the claim that love is the only law, the ideal of purity loses its importance.

GIANNI VATTIMO: This becomes more and more true today because all these ideas of purity and sexual morality are applied by the Church to the questions of bioethics, therefore it becomes more meaningful since people do not care much about sexual impurity even of the priests. But when it comes to the modification of DNA, the importance of the question becomes more evident and so does the absurdity of the Church attitude. It might be bioethics that will kill the sexual attitude of the Church.

RICHARD RORTY: Perhaps, yes.

GIANNI VATTIMO: Even the question of prohibiting prophylactics in this time of AIDS: it's absurd, but the pope cannot say so because otherwise he would go against the Church.

RICHARD RORTY: Yes. If he would announce that, it would mean he was admitting that there is no such thing as "natural" sexuality.

GIANNI VATTIMO: This is a very important point. From one point of view it is always *mauvais goût*, bad taste, to reproach the Church for being against homosexuals because it seems to be to *chercher la bagarre* [spoiling for a fight], but it is an important point to criticize this naturalistic attitude.

RICHARD RORTY: Derrida's importance in the history of philosophy may turn out to be having been the first guy who brought Freud and Heidegger together. This enables him to move back and forth, humorously, between sex and metaphysics. His work helps us see the connection between the two and thus to better understand the role of the churches.

SANTIAGO ZABALA: So the future of religion will depend on a position which is "beyond atheism and theism"?

GIANNI VATTIMO: Yes, in a way of being a guide without the eschatology of Hegel, without the idea we have reached the culminating point. During these days we are celebrating in Italy the fiftieth anniversary of Benedetto Croce. He died in December 1952, when I was still a high school student. I have understood better and better Gadamer's idea that we can be Hegelian by stopping the system of the objective spirit and Croce's idea that we have to substitute for the culmination of Hegel a sort of "historical spirit"; this is also what his reform consisted of. It's always the same at the end, the true being is *Geist*, but *Geist* does not conclude its history in a sort of Cartesian self evidence, but in something different.

RICHARD RORTY: It's also the fiftieth anniversary of Dewey's death. He had the same noneschatological version of

Hegel as Croce. Dewey would, I think, have agreed with practically everything Croce said in his book *What is Living and What is Dead in the Philosophy of Hegel.*

GIANNI VATTIMO: In Italy we have the strangest phenomenon. Of the two greatest Italians philosophers, of the first part of the twentieth century, Gentile and Croce, it was Gentile who was always considered a better philosopher, but only by the people who opposed him, by the realist philosophers of the Catholic University of Milan. They expanded and preached the idea that Gentile was the realist secular philosopher of Italy since he was much easier to object to because he always spoke of the *actus purus,* the pure act, to which he reduced everything. This was like a sort of Berkeleyian idealism: everything is in our consciousness! Even if he was very radical, nothing really happened, since this thesis can't really be defended practically; it was a sort of continuation of the revolution of D'Annunzio's esthetic view of politics. Croce instead was much more respectful of creations of the spirit; he did not think that art was dead. As to religion, I don't know what he thought. But his dialectical concluding point was a very interesting idea, which perhaps is a "true" point of pragmatism. Anyway, religion is not dead, Santiago, God is still around . . .

Notes

1. The discussion Rorty refers to here is also pursued in chapters 6 and 7 of Robert Brandom's *Tales of the Mighty Dead: Historical Essays in the Metaphysics of Intentionality* (Cambridge, Mass.: Harvard University Press, 2002).

2. In Gianni Vattimo, *Nihilism and Emancipation. Ethics, Politics, and Law,* ed. Santiago Zabala, trans. William McCuaig (New York: Columbia University Press, in press).

Contributors

Richard Rorty is professor of comparative literature and philosophy at Stanford University. His books include *The Linguistic Turn*; *Philosophy and the Mirror of Nature*; *Consequences of Pragmatism*; *Contingency, Irony, and Solidarity*; *Objectivity, Relativism, and Truth: Philosophical Papers I*; *Essays on Heidegger and Others: Philosophical Papers II*; *Truth, Politics, and Post-Modernism*; *Achieving Our Country*; *Truth and Progress: Philosophical Papers III*; and *Philosophy and Social Hope*.

Gianni Vattimo teaches theoretical and hermeneutical philosophy at the University of Turin. His books in English include

The End of Modernity; The Adventure of Difference; The Transparent Society; Secularization of Philosophy; Nietzsche: An Introduction; Beyond Interpretation; Belief; Religion (with J. Derrida); *After Christianity;* and *Nihilism and Emancipation.*

Santiago Zabala is researcher in philosophy at the Pontifical Lateran University of Rome. He is the author of numerous publications on religion and postmodern thought. He has edited Gianni Vattimo's *Nihilism and Emancipation* and is now preparing and editing *Weakening Philosophy: Festschrift in Honour of Gianni Vattimo* with contributions from distinguished philosophers.

INDEX

arbitrariness, 59
atheism, 6–7, 32–34
atheist, as term, 30
authenticity, of interpretation,
    44–45
authoritarianism, 8–9, 50, 68–69

Being, 3, 20–21n. 5, 23n. 10, 45;
    beings identified with, 5, 77;
    as event, 61, 62, 66; historicity
    of, 44, 62; as language, 56, 57;
    pragmatic approach to, 57–58;
    as result of dialogue, 66–67;
    weakening of, 19n. 4, 23n. 10
Being and Time (Heidegger), 30,
    44
belief, 24n. 11, 24–25n. 14,
    32–34
Berlin, Isaiah, 60
biblical references: 1 Corinthians
    13, 35, 39, 40; Epistle to the
    Romans, 35; Gospel according
    to John, 68; John 8.32, 14
biblical tradition, 17–18, 45,
    53–54, 77–78
Bildung, 4, 6–7, 18n. 2
bioethics, 15, 48, 79
Bloom, Harold, 70
Brandom, Robert, 37, 56, 58, 68

capitalism, 74–75
Cartesian thought, 36–37
Catholic Church. *See* Church
Catholic University of Milan, 81
charity/love, 6, 12, 38, 56, 59,
    76; history and, 35–36; linked
    with truth, 13, 50–51
China, ancient, 64
Christ, 17, 38, 46. *See also* Incar-
    nation/*kenosis*

Christianity: antimetaphysical
    consequences, 6, 14, 53,
    61–62; charity/love as message
    of, 50–51, 56; democracy and,
    73–74; denial of reality prin-
    ciple, 49–50; function of in
    postmodern condition, 15–16;
    historicity of, 53–54; interiority
    and, 17, 46–47; laic vocation,
    7, 13, 15; message of, 17,
    49–52, 66; missionary compo-
    nent, 15, 65–66; nihilism as
    truth of, 47, 51; as not yet
    nihilistic enough, 61–62, 67,
    78–79; salvific message, 52
Church: authoritarianism of,
    68–69; future of, 2, 69–70;
    literalism of, 48–49; natural
    law approach, 48–49, 80;
    project to prove objectivity,
    14–15; sexuality, position on,
    15–16, 79–80; structure of,
    68–69
civic responsibility, 72
civilization, as mission, 72
classics, 53, 60–61
Common Faith, A (Dewey), 78
common life, 67
commonsensical secularism,
    26–27n. 16
communicative reason, 30
community, 51
Comte, Auguste, 69
Confucian tradition, 64
consensus, dialogical, 23n. 7
contextual traditions, 78–79
continuity, 58–59, 61
Contribution to Philosophy (Heideg-
    ger), 65
conversational philosophy, 68